TASTE OF THE
PACIFIC

Susan Parkinson
Peggy Stacy & Adrian Mattinson

Warwick Publishing

Toronto   Los Angeles

We acknowledge the following books used for research of motif material:
Patterns of Polynesia: The Cook Islands, Ailsa Robertson, Heinemann Education (1989)
Patterns of Polynesia: Samoa, Ailsa Robertson, Heinemann Education (1989)

Published in June 1996 by:
Warwick Publishing Inc.,
24 Mercer Street, Suite 200, Toronto, Ontario M5V 1H3
1424 N. Highland Avenue, Los Angeles, CA 90027

Distributed in North America by:
Firefly Books Ltd.,
3680 Victoria Park Avenue, Willowdale, Ontario M2H 3K1

ISBN 1-895629-66-7

First published in 1985 as *Taste of the Tropics*
Second edition published in 1989 by
David Bateman Ltd.,
Auckland, New Zealand

A completely revised and redesigned edition published in 1995 by
David Bateman Ltd.

Photography by Ron Redfern (except pages 56 & 57 by Jason Stacy)
Design by Errol McLeary
Cover design by Diane Farenick
Typeset in New Century Schoolbook and Bodoni bold condensed
Printed in Hong Kong by Colorcraft

CONTENTS

The authors

Susan Parkinson, a home economist and dietitian, worked in New Zealand and England before gaining a Masters degree in nutrition at Cornell University, USA. Since 1950 she has lived in the South Pacific where she has been involved in developing Fiji and regional nutrition programmes. Her publications include a hotel cookery book; *A Professional Guide to Fiji Produce,* written for the Tourism Council of the South Pacific, *The Pacific Island's Nutrition Handbook;* and with A.A. Jansen and A. Robertson, *Food and Nutrition in Fiji,* together with numerous scientific papers and popular articles on food and nutrition.

With **Peggy Stacy** she developed an interest in adapting traditional Islands foods for use by rising urban populations and for inclusion in international cuisine. Their first book, *Taste of the Tropics,* 1972, was sold throughout the tropical world; and in 1977 the *Pacific Islands Cook Book* was written for urban islanders.

In 1985 she was awarded the Order of the British Empire for services to Fiji.

Peggy Stacy is a qualified dietitian trained in Canada and the USA. She is a member of the Australian Dietetic Association and the Nutrition Society. She has been co-author of numerous books, such as the *Best Australian Cookbook for Diabetics* and *The Overweight and the Family Diet Cookbook.* Peggy now lives in Perth, Australia, with her family, where she presently lectures, consults and runs seminars while continuing recipe development.

Adrian Mattinson has built up wide experience in hotel and food management since graduating from the Scottish Hotel School. Born in England, he followed an international career in the management of hotels and their food and beverage departments, in countries as diverse as the Seychelles, West Africa and the Caribbean. He spent four years in Fiji, partly as Head of the School of Hotel and Catering Services in Suva, and partly running a group of four hotels. He was co-author of *Taste of the Tropics* with Susan and Peggy.

Adrian emigrated to New Zealand in 1986 and after a further period in hotel management education is currently Passenger Services Manager for New Zealand Rail's Interisland Line.

Susan Parkinson

Peggy Stacy

Adrian Mattinson

Acknowledgements

Our grateful thanks to the following:
Carolyn Tiffin for help in adapting the manuscript for use in North America.
Ron Redfern for the photography.
Mr. Y.P. Reddy and staff of the Tanoa Group of Hotels, Fiji, for their assistance and interest.
The Tourism Council of the South Pacific for permission to use recipes from a *Professional Guide to Fiji Produce.*
The National Marketing Authority of Fiji for providing fresh produce for recipe testing and photographic assistance.
Robert Stone for information on gamefish.
Meredani Nuibalavu for recipe assistance.
Nutrition Department, University of Otago, New Zealand, for information on nutrition and coconuts.
Fiji National Food and Nutrition Committee for general assistance.
New Zealand Institute for Crop & Food Research for additional information on food composition.
Pat Mattinson for proofing and for her eternal patience.
Janet Bateman for her untiring editorial assistance.
The South Pacific Trade Commission (SPTC) for their invaluable assistance.

Weights and measures

Imperial and metric weights and measures are given. Where possible, ingredients are measured in standard cups 8 fl. oz (250 ml), teaspoons (5 ml), tablespoons (15 ml). All these measurements are level.

Approximate metric conversion table

25 g = 1 oz
400 g = 1 lb
1 kg = 2.2 lb
1 liter = 1.05 quarts U.S.
1 liter = 4 standard cups
1 standard cup + 8 fl oz (250 ml)
2.5 cm = 1 inch

Metric abbreviations

mm = millimeter
cm = centimeter
g = gram
kg = kilogram
ml = milliliter
C = celsius
F = fahrenheit

Oven temperatures

	°F	°C	Gas
Very slow	200	100	¼
	220	110	½
	250	120	¾
Slow	275	140	2
Moderately slow	300	150	3
Moderate	350	180	4
Moderately hot	375	190	5
	400	200	6
Hot	425	220	7
Very hot	450	230	8
	475	250	9

Introduction

This cookbook and guide to tropical fruits and vegetables has its foundation in the very successful *Taste of the Tropics* which, from the 1970s, encouraged thousands of people in many different countries to sample and enjoy tropical foods.

It gains its inspiration from the numerous island nations of the tropical Pacific, a gastronomic and cultural melting pot which has evolved through thousands of years of migration, colonization, and now, independent nationhood. The authors have spent many years living, working and travelling in these magnificently diverse islands.

The foods of the Pacific Islands, rich in produce from the sea, coconuts grown on coral beaches, fruits and vegetables from village gardens and plantations, are found in most tropical countries. Ever-improving harvest and storage techniques, together with the speed of modern transport, bring many of these exciting and nutritious products to markets all over the world. They add a new dimension to our daily fare by providing excitement to the palate and an unending challenge to the innovative cook.

Residents of the Pacific Islands are now benefitting from advanced growing techniques, such as hydroponics, which make available to them many temperate vegetables and fruits which expand their daily menus. The recipes in this book show the influence of these changes in food availability.

The success of a tropical culinary adventure depends on the understanding and correct use of these foods. To do this, we give you easy and quick-to-prepare recipes for all occasions. In case you cannot find all the ingredients, we have suggested some suitable temperate climate alternatives. At the back of the book you will find a *Tropical Fruit and Vegetable Guide*, which gives advice on the selection, use, storage and nutritive value of a comprehensive selection of tropical fruits and vegetables.

For some readers, this book and its recipes will be a happy reminder of vacations spent in tropical countries; for others, it will undoubtedly provide a spur to travel to our part of the world. We hope that all who use the book will enjoy expanding their culinary horizons.

This book is intended not only for people living in areas with sophisticated and comprehensive supplies, but also for those in more remote areas where ingenuity and adaptation of recipes to local supplies and conditions apply.

Guide to preparing Pacific Island foods

Before you embark on your culinary adventure, it is very important that you read this part of the book which gives you essential information on the use and nutritional values of, and substitutes for, ingredients which occur frequently throughout the book.

Coconut

Coconut, in all its forms, has provided, for thousands of years, the main source of fat for people living in many tropical countries around the world. It provides a distinctive and irreplaceable flavor and texture to numerous Pacific Island and Southeast Asian recipes.

Coconuts are normally eaten with a variety of other foods in the Pacific. Besides enhancing the flavor of food, the fat aids the utilization of fat-soluble vitamins from vegetables and fruits, whilst the flesh provides an important source of fiber. Although coconut cream is made up of saturated fats, the food alone does not raise or lower blood cholesterol levels. This is due to the type of fatty acid found in coconuts.

However, if the daily food eaten contains a lot of other saturated fats from animal foods, like butter and bacon, the addition of coconut could increase the total saturated fat content of the diet and lead to a rise in blood cholesterol levels.

Cooking with coconut

Thick and thin coconut cream may be compared to double and single cream in calorie value and for this reason should be eaten in moderation. You can enjoy coconut cream flavor with reduced calorific value by diluting as follows:

* Blending equal parts of coconut cream with either reduced fat 'light or low fat' sour cream or cream cheese.
* Adding double the specified quantity of water when preparing fresh coconut cream, or when preparing coconut cream from dried coconut cream powder; or by diluting canned coconut cream.
* Adding unsweetened fruit juice or coconut water to prepared coconut cream.

Coconut cream contains some protein. When boiled, the protein curdles and separates out. This does not matter in some dishes, but in other recipes, such as fish soup, the consistency and flavor are spoiled by boiling the cream.

To prevent curdling, add between 1 teaspoon and 1 tablespoon of cornstarch to each cup of coconut cream, (depending on required consistency and recipe), and bring to the boil, stirring constantly, before including in the recipe.

How to open a fresh coconut

A fresh, mature coconut is brown in color, and should feel heavy. When shaken, the juice should 'rattle.' The fibrous shell should be dry, particularly around the 'eyes.' When opened the flesh is firm and white.

To open, firstly drain all the juice, or coconut water, by piercing an 'eye' with a skewer. Choose one of the rib lines that run from the 'eyes' to the other end of the nut and tap sharply across the middle of the line with a heavy knife or cleaver. The nut should split evenly into two halves, but do take care with this action!

Save the juice or coconut water which, when chilled, is a refreshing drink, or use when making coconut cream. To remove the flesh, use a round-ended knife, slicing in a circular manner — not lengthwise. The flesh will come out easily.

Green coconuts

These are prized for the sweet juice and gelatinous flesh. The juice is an important drink and the flesh is included in desserts and used as an infant food.

Germinating coconuts

The sprouting nut has a soft 'ball' inside, sometimes known as the coconut apple. This is a popular food with children and is also used in the preparation of special drinks and desserts.

Coconut cream

How to make coconut cream

This essential ingredient of tropical cooking is best made from fresh nuts, but if not available, canned or powdered coconut cream provides an excellent substitute.

To make the cream, first grate the flesh with a hand grater or use a blender or food processor. Mix 1 cup warm water with 1 cup of grated flesh. Knead the mixture for 1 minute. If using a blender or food processor, place 1 cup of cut flesh with 1 cup of warm water in the blender and blend at high speed until completely pulverised.

Put the blended or hand-kneaded flesh into a piece of cheese cloth or muslin and squeeze out the cream into a bowl.

For a thinner cream, repeat the process in the blender or bowl, using the squeezed flesh and another cup of water.

For very thick cream use no water (or just half a cup) when blending or kneading the fresh nut flesh.

How to open a fresh coconut

Storage of coconut cream

Coconut cream may be frozen in containers or cubes. After defrosting, beat well before using.

The cream quickly solidifies in a refrigerator. Take out and put the container into a bowl of warm water and beat well before using. The cream will last for 1–2 days if refrigerated.

Canned coconut cream

This may be used in place of fresh cream in any recipe. Always shake the can well before opening, as the cream tends to rise to the top.

Some recipes require the use of thick coconut cream. To attain this, allow the can to stand, then open carefully and pour off the creamy top half of the liquid.

Powdered coconut cream

This is an excellent product which should be prepared according to the instructions on the packet. It is particularly useful when small quantities of coconut cream are required in a recipe.

Other coconut products

Fermented coconut or coconut cheese

This delicious product is made by using a process similar to that used for making dairy cheese. It is used to flavor vegetable and seaweed dishes, and it is sometimes cooked with fish. It can also be used as a flavorsome alternative to cream cheese.

Traditionally, the Fijians ferment fresh coconut in the sea to make a product called 'kora.' Kora can also be made by using modern fermentation methods.

Coconut syrup and sugar

In the Micronesian Islands this is made by collecting juice from the cut stem of the coconut flower. The juice is then evaporated to form a syrup similar in texture to maple syrup. In Southeast Asia, the syrup is further reduced to make a form of sugar.

Coconut flower juice is an important health drink in Micronesia and it is also fermented to make beer. In many parts of southern Asia it is further distilled to make 'arrack.'

Grated coconut

Fresh coconut flesh may be grated on a hand grater, or broken into pieces and then blended in a food processor using the stainless steel chopping blade. Avoid, if possible, the outer brown skin, and you will get a finer grind. Adding a little liquid to the mixture will make the grating much easier. Grate to the consistency you want. For cake and dessert toppings, it is best not to grate the flesh too finely.

Grated coconut will keep for 1–2 days in the refrigerator in a plastic bag. Add hot water before squeezing to make cream. It may also be frozen.

Substitute for fresh coconut

Freshly grated coconut may be replaced with desiccated coconut. Allow ¾ cup of desiccated coconut mixed with ¼ cup of warm water to replace 1 cup of fresh nut flesh. Mix thoroughly and leave for a short time to allow the dry coconut to absorb the water.

Use of coconut in cool climates

Coconut cream becomes solid at a higher temperature than most cooking oils. To liquefy canned cream, place the can in warm water before using. Freshly grated coconut should be warmed to room temperature before squeezing out cream — alternatively add warm water to the grated flesh.

Yogurt

Yogurt is an essential part of Indian and Middle East cooking. It adds an acid flavor which helps to tenderise tough meat and aids digestion.

How to make your own yogurt

2½ cups milk
2 tablespoons dried skim milk
4 tablespoons commercial or home-made yogurt

Heat milk until just below boiling point or until it is frothy, but not boiling. Cool to body temperature. Remove the skin from the surface of the milk. Add 1 cup of heated milk slowly to the skim milk powder. Combine remaining warm milk with the skim milk mixture and yogurt. Put into a clean jar and leave to set in a warm place; alternatively, pour into a wide mouthed Thermos flask. When set, store in the refrigerator.

Low fat yogurt

Use skim milk instead of full cream milk.

Thick yogurt

2 cups milk
1 cup skim milk powder
4 tablespoons commercial or home-made yogurt

Prepare as for plain yogurt.

The many uses of yogurt

Yogurt provides the base for many sauces such as raita (page 25) and is an excellent addition to both bland and spicy dishes and soups. Thick yogurt may be used as a substitute for cream. Beat until smooth and add the desired flavor before serving as a topping, garnish or salad dressing. A refreshing sauce for desserts or salads is made by slowly beating equal quantities of low fat yogurt and cream. This produces a flavor similar to crème fraîche.

To prevent yogurt from curdling during cooking, add 1 tablespoon of cornstarch, mixed to a paste with a little yoghurt, to every cup of yogurt. Bring to the boil, stirring all the time, before blending into your recipe.

7

Chop or slice fresh pineapple, mango, papaya or other tropical fruits and add to yogurt to make your own tropical fruit-flavored yogurt. It is also delicious using a mixture of chopped crystallised tropical fruit and chopped macadamia or cashew nuts.

Fats and oils

In many recipes we have quoted the use of butter or margarine. However, in almost all cases these can be substituted with your favorite shortening.

For health reasons, vegetable oils and fats, (such as polyunsaturated margarine), should be used wherever possible. However, there are certain dishes where the distinctive flavor and richness of butter is essential. To retain some of the butter flavor, it is possible to use half butter and half vegetable oil in recipes such as those requiring a roux-based sauce, or for sautéing.

Ghee is clarified butter. It is important in Indian cooking where its use contributes to the fine flavor of curries, pilaus and other dishes. It is a pure butter fat with no milk solids and can therefore be heated to a higher temperature than ordinary butter without burning.

Vegetable oils are included in many of our recipes. We suggest that you use the oil of your choice and for this reason we do not often specify one particular type. However, recipes in this book were tested using corn oil. It is recommended that you experiment by flavoring oils with your favorite herbs and spices. A particularly good one for general use is olive oil in which whole cloves of garlic (1 per cup of oil), bay leaves and small whole chilies (1 per cup of oil) are marinated.

Banana leaf cooking

The banana leaf provides an ideal covering for cooking food, by helping to retain the flavor and juices of fish, chicken, beef and vegetables. Banana leaves also impart a special flavor of their own which cannot be achieved

How to cut fresh pineapple

Firstly cut off the top and base of the pineapple and peel off the outer skin with a sharp knife. Then starting at the top, make parallel cuts in the form of a wedge on each side of the 'eyes', working down around the pineapple in a spiral manner. When completed, there should be a series of ridges running round from top to bottom with no 'eyes' left.

The pineapple is now ready for slicing or dicing, depending on how you wish to serve it.

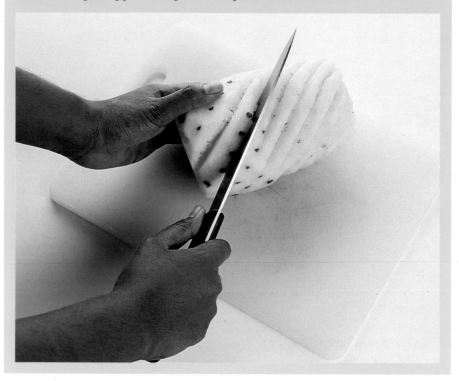

when aluminium foil is used as a substitute.

Preparing the leaf

To prepare banana leaf for wrapping food, first select a young whole leaf. With a sharp knife, slice off the thick vein on the back and then hold the leaf over a flame or hot coals. Move it backwards and forwards until soft and pliable. Wrap the food in the leaf and tie with cotton or a strip of fiber made from the sliced off leaf vein.

Microwave note*:* The banana leaf makes an ideal cover for food cooked in the microwave oven. This may be used in place of plastic wrap or a covering dish.

Taro (rourou) leaves

These leaves should be boiled for at least 10 minutes in water or coconut milk as they contain a substance which may irritate the mouth.

Rice cooking

Rice is an important ingredient in many tropical recipes. A number of meat and vegetable dishes are also served with rice. Different types of rice are used by people living in tropical countries. Some people prefer the rounder grained types which have a stickier texture, whilst others like the drier long grained varieties.

In our recipes we have used long grain rice which, when properly cooked, should have a light fluffy appearance. In all our recipes we suggest that the rice is washed thoroughly before use. This is particularly important for rice purchased in parts of the world where it is not cleaned before being packed. Washing removes impurities and surplus starch. However, it is not necessary to wash any clean processed rice that is purchased in sealed packets.

We recommend the following three methods of cooking rice:

1. The Asian way is to wash the rice and then place in a pot, adding 2 cups of water for each cup of rice. Add salt to taste and bring to the boil. Boil for 5 minutes, cover with a lid and steam over a very low heat until the grains are soft. Loosen with a fork. This is similar to the method used with automatic electric rice cookers.
2. Alternatively, boil 8 cups of water and sprinkle 1 cup of washed rice into the boiling water, adding salt to taste. Boil for about 10 minutes or until just soft. Strain, rinse in cold water and then steam over a pot of boiling water in a colander to make it fluffier.
3. For rice cooked in a microwave, allow 10–12 minutes to cook 1 cup of rice. Put rice into a casserole. Add 2 cups of warm water to 1 cup of washed rice and ¼ teaspoon of salt. Cover and cook on high for 10-12 minutes. Stand for 5 minutes.

Microwave cooking for tropical dishes

This is an efficient way of cooking a number of tropical foods. Through-out the book we have recommended use of a microwave as an alternative method for cooking selected recipes. We have found that spicy curries, rice dishes, recipes containing coconut cream, fish and vegetables respond particularly well to this method of cooking.

However, some tropical vegetables such as root crops, breadfruit and taro leaves, do not respond well to microwave cooking.

Recipes were tested in a 650 watt microwave oven with a revolving plate. We suggest that the recommended cooking times be used only as a guide. You will find that these vary slightly according to the type of oven, temperature of food and cooking containers.

Spices

Spices are an essential part of many tropical dishes. Getting the best results from these wonderfully aromatic and flavorsome additions, depends on knowing how to select, prepare, use and store them.

Preparation of spices

When bought loose, always wash and then dry in the sun or a warm oven until crisp. Store in airtight containers. For long storage, keep in the refrigerator or freezer, ensuring that they are sealed to avoid scent transference to other foods. Grind spices using a spice or coffee grinder. Always clean the grinder after each use to remove flavors.

When using whole spices like cloves and cinnamon sticks, bruise the spices with a heavy spoon to release the flavor. In curries, pilaus and similar dishes, spices are sautéed in oil, ghee or butter on a low or medium heat to develop the flavors. Care must be taken not to overheat the oil or ghee as this will spoil the spices.

Large pieces of whole spice may be removed before serving to improve the appearance of the dish. Smaller spices like cardamom and cumin seeds may be left in dishes.

Masala

Masala is a basic mixture of spices which varies greatly according to individual tastes and to different regions of India. When turmeric is added it is known as curry (or kari) powder. A simple masala would be coriander and peppercorns, ground and blended, using about three times as much coriander as black pepper. Other masalas could be coriander, fenugreek and mustard seed; or coriander, peppercorns, cinnamon, cumin and fennel seed. For example:

3 tablespoons coriander seeds
1 tablespoon cumin seeds
1 tablespoon black peppercorns
1 tablespoon mustard seed
1 tablespoon cloves
1 tablespoon turmeric
1 tablespoon ground ginger or freshly ground ginger root

Grind all the whole spices and blend with turmeric and ground ginger.

Garam masala

This is a fragrant, strong mixture which is suitable for meat, fried or braised, and in small quantities with vegetables.

6 tablespoons black peppercorns
5 tablespoons caraway seeds
1¾ tablespoons cinnamon stick
6 tablespoons dried coriander
1¾ tablespoons cloves
1½ tablespoons cardamom seeds

Grind and blend all ingredients. Store in an airtight jar.

Tamarind

This is the acid fruit of a tropical tree. Bean-like fruits are covered in a soft brown flesh. Tamarind is dried to a date-like consistency and sold in packets. To use, soak about 1 tablespoonful in ½ cup of hot water for ten minutes and then squeeze through a strainer. The liquid is then used to impart an acid flavor to food and drinks. More concentrated instant forms are also available.

Further notes

Flour

Unless specified we have used All Purpose Flour. However, you may like to try your favorite flour — or a mix of different flours to produce a tastier, or more unusual taste and texture.

Sugar

Plain white sugar is used except where specified. However, if you use raw sugar or similar, it is important that the strong caramel and molasses flavors do not unbalance the taste of the finished dish.

Gelatine

In all recipes unflavored gelatine is used.

APPETIZERS
DIPS & CHIPS
COCKTAILS & SAUCES

Making your own appetizers is not as difficult or as time-consuming as you may think — and they taste so much better.

Although you can make your own short or choux pastry cases, there are many excellent commercially produced cases and canapé bases available, which can be stored in airtight containers. It is, however, very important that the case or base you use is fairly bland in taste so that it does not interfere with the flavor of the filling or topping. Excellent bases can be made by toasting or baking, in a low oven, thin slices of French bread (baguette), or trimmed squares or shapes of white, wholemeal, rye or pumpernickel bread.

Reduced fat cream cheese makes an excellent and receptive base for a number of different cold toppings.

A seasoned white sauce, made the day before and chilled, can be mixed with a variety of different flavorings and spooned into the prepared cases when required.

Savories requiring last minute baking or broiling can also be made well ahead and deep frozen. These should heated in the oven, under the broiler, or in the microwave, just before serving.

Fillings for pastry cases

Pastry cases of differing shapes and sizes may be filled with any of the following mixtures which are based on a white sauce. The size of the case depends on how much filling is used, but it is important that the cases are dainty and usually 1 teaspoon of filling is sufficient. These mixtures also make delicious crêpe fillings.

White sauce

3 tablespoons butter or margarine
½ clove garlic, crushed
3 tablespoons flour
1 cup milk
¼ teaspoon dry mustard
salt
dash pepper

Melt butter in a saucepan and gently sauté garlic. Stir in flour, ensuring it is well blended with the butter. Allow to gently cook for about 2 minutes before gradually adding the boiled milk. Add mustard powder and cook over a low heat until thick and smooth, stirring often, about 3 minutes. Adjust seasoning.
Yield: 1½ cups.

Microwave note: Put butter in a 4-cup (1-liter) glass measure. Add garlic, pepper and mustard. Microwave on high uncovered for one minute. Stir in flour and salt. Microwave on high for 30 seconds. Slowly stir in milk and blend well. Microwave on high for 3½–4 minutes, stirring every minute until the sauce is thick and bubbling.

Low fat white sauce

1 cup milk, standard or low fat
½ small onion, peeled and left
** whole**
1 bay leaf
2 tablespoons cornstarch
salt

Heat milk in a saucepan with onion and bay leaf, retaining 1 tablespoon of milk to blend with the cornstarch into a smooth paste. When milk is just below boiling point, remove the onion and bay leaf, and stir in cornstarch, milk paste and salt to taste. Allow mixture to thicken but not boil, stirring constantly. The consistency of this base sauce can be adjusted by reducing or increasing the amount of cornstarch used.

Chili crab filling

1½ cups white sauce (page 10)
1 large clove garlic, finely
** chopped**
1 tablespoon butter or margarine
1 cup cooked or canned crab,
** coarsely flaked**
2 teaspoons chili or Tabasco sauce
2 teaspoons lemon juice
2 tablespoons finely chopped
** parsley or 2 teaspoons dried**
** parsley**
salt

Prepare white sauce. Sauté garlic in butter, stir in crab and cook for 3 minutes. Add chili sauce, lemon juice and parsley. Cook for 1 minute. Stir in white sauce and check seasoning.
Yield: 2 cups.

Left to right: Chili crab garnished with prawns, South seas filling, petite drumsticks and chili crab filling

South seas filling

**½ cup marinated fish fillets (fresh
or frozen cod or snapper)**
1 cup coconut cream (page 6)
2 teaspoons cornstarch
1 tablespoon lemon juice
salt
dash chili or Tabasco sauce
**½ teaspoon ground nutmeg or
allspice**
¼ cup finely chopped cucumber

Prepare marinated fish fillet as for kokoda (page 16). Prepare coconut cream (page 6), or if unavailable use canned, unsweetened coconut cream. Pour ¾ cup coconut cream into a saucepan. Mix cornstarch into the remaining ¼ cup and then blend together in the saucepan. Stir constantly over a medium heat until the mixture is thickened but do not

allow to boil. Remove from heat and add lemon juice, salt, chili and nutmeg.

Fold in the drained fish. Just before filling pastry cases, add the cucumber. Serve hot.
Yield: 2 cups.

Petite drumsticks

2 lb (800 g) chicken wings
2 eggs, well beaten
¼ cup flour
1 teaspoon salt
1 tablespoon dry sherry
vegetable oil for deep-frying
**freshly ground pepper or chili
powder**

To form the petite drumsticks, using a sharp knife cut wings at joints into 2 sections and discard tips. Separate the two bones of the first section,

being careful to leave the flesh attached to the bone. With the tip of the knife, lift the flesh from one end of the bone and push it towards the other end to form the petite drumstick. (Two sections of wing yield 3 drumsticks. However, in more sophisticated shopping areas, it may be possible to buy drumsticks already prepared.)

In a bowl, mix the eggs, flour, salt and sherry. Dip the drumsticks in the batter and deep-fry a few at a time, in hot oil at 370°F (190°C), until crisp and golden. Drain well on paper towel and sprinkle with freshly ground pepper or a little chili powder. Serve hot.

Note: Can be prepared in advance and chilled. Refry for 2–3 minutes before serving.

11

Tropical vegetable and fruit terrine

The brilliance of color and variation of texture make this terrine well worth the effort. It keeps well chilled and can be frozen either whole, or sliced and interleaved with pieces of lightly oiled waxed paper. Because of the nature of this dish, it is impractical to make in smaller quantities so this recipe is intended for use at a buffet or to be used portioned and frozen.

Selection of up to five vegetables and one fruit, chosen for their color and texture differences, (long beans, purple kumara, sweet potato, tomato, taro leaves and mango). The total amount, trimmed and prepared should be 5 cups
1 cup double cream or crème fraîche
1 cup low fat sour cream
1 cup coconut cream
2 teaspoons finely chopped fresh ginger root
1 teaspoon crushed green peppercorns
salt
½ cup sliced mushrooms
1½ tablespoons gelatine
boiling water
1 cup soft white breadcrumbs
2 tablespoons dry vermouth

Carefully select the vegetables to provide for a layer of each in a 8-cup (2-liter) terrine or bread mold. Cut the root crops in lengths and into a cross-section of different shapes, such as diamonds or squares. Cook lightly. Wash off excess starch, drain and leave to cool. If using taro leaves, simmer whole leaves, with central spines removed, for at least 10 minutes. Peel and de-seed the tomatoes and cut into small cubes. Cut the mango into thin strips. When prepared put into the refrigerator. Whisk together cream, sour cream and coconut cream, add ginger root, peppercorns, salt and sliced, washed mushrooms. Heat but do not boil. Dissolve gelatine in a small amount of boiling water and add to the mixture. After 10 minutes remove the mushrooms and discard.

Add the white breadcrumbs and dry vermouth, stirring constantly.

Pour a little cream liquid into a lightly greased or Teflon-coated mold and then place alternate layers of taro leaves and other vegetables and fruit, pouring in the liquid so that the level remains constant. When complete, tap the mold lightly to ensure all vegetables and fruit have settled and then refrigerate for at least 6 hours before serving.

Turn out onto a plate or cutting board and serve, suitably decorated. This terrine is delicious with an unsweetened purée of papaya or pineapple.
Yield: 15 portions.

Chicken liver and vegetable pâté

The basic ingredients of the traditional French pâté are finely chopped liver or pork combined with a good deal of fat and fine flavorings. In this recipe, we reduce the calories by including vegetables and less fat. The mixture should be chilled in a mold overnight, sliced and served as an appetizer with toast. It can also be used as a party spread.

3 cups mixed cut-up vegetables (beans, peas, carrots, eggplant)
2 tablespoons margarine
1 tablespoon butter
½ medium onion, finely chopped
½ clove garlic, crushed
1 teaspoon freshly ground black pepper
½ teaspoon ground nutmeg
10 oz (250 g) chicken livers, chopped
½ cup chopped mushrooms
2 teaspoons gelatine
1 tablespoon water
¼ teaspoon French or Dijon mustard
¼ cup brandy or dry sherry
salt

Boil the vegetables quickly in a small amount of water and drain, or microwave on high for 6–8 minutes.

Melt the margarine and butter and sauté the onion, garlic, pepper, mustard and nutmeg until the onion is lightly cooked. Add chicken livers

and stir-fry over a medium heat. Add mushrooms and cook for about 2 minutes. Mix gelatine with water and add to livers. Stir thoroughly to melt evenly. Put all ingredients in a food processor or blender, or mince together. Stir brandy or sherry into finely chopped mixture. Set in a mold overnight. Turn out and serve, suitably garnished.
Yield: 2 cups.

Luau (taro leaf) seafood pâté

This colorful and tasty pâté is easy to make and keeps well chilled or frozen. The idea for the recipe comes from a traditional Tongan method of cooking taro leaves with cornstarch and coconut cream.

½ lb (200 g) taro leaves
½ cup water or fish stock
¼ cup finely chopped onion
½ teaspoon crushed garlic
½ teaspoon crushed green ginger root
salt
3 tablespoons cornstarch
¼ cup thick coconut cream
3 teaspoons gelatine
2 tablespoons water
8 oz (200 g) good quality fish fillets
¼ cup fish or vegetable stock
bay leaf

Cut up taro leaves and put in a saucepan with stock or water, onion, garlic, ginger and salt. Boil with lid off for at least 10 minutes. Mix cornstarch with coconut cream and combine with a little of the hot mixture before adding to the taro leaves. Stirring all the time, simmer until cornstarch is cooked, about 3–4 minutes. Soften gelatine in water and stir into hot mixture. Remove from heat, cool and blend, or rub through a strainer.

Simmer fish fillets in stock with bay leaf until soft, about 4–5 minutes, or microwave, covered, on medium heat for 4 minutes. Purée fish with stock, either using a blender or through a strainer. Fold into taro leaf mixture. Set in a mold.
Yield: 2 cups.

Variation: In place of fish use 16½-oz (185-g) can flaked tuna. Also makes attractive canapés when served on toast squares garnished with a piece of prawn and a tiny lemon wedge.

Red bean pâté

A good vegetarian spread.

1 small onion, finely chopped
1 clove garlic, crushed
1 tablespoon vegetable oil
1 cup cooked and drained kidney beans
1 tablespoon tomato paste or 2 tablespoons tomato purée
1 teaspoon chopped fresh basil or ½ teaspoon dried basil
salt
1 tablespoon sherry (optional)
water or stock

Note: If using raw beans, soak in cold water for 2 hours. Drain, add fresh water and boil until soft.

In a saucepan sauté onion and garlic in the oil. Stir in kidney beans, tomato paste and basil. Simmer for 3 minutes.

Purée in a blender or food processor. Add salt and mix in sherry if desired.

To adjust the consistency of the spread, add a small amount of water or stock. Chill overnight to blend flavors.
Yield: 1½ cups.

Spicy chicken and plantain filling

1 tablespoon vegetable oil
1 teaspoon garam masala (page 9)
½ cup finely sliced green onion
¾ cup finely chopped plantain or unripe banana
salt
1 cup finely chopped raw chicken breast
½ tablespoon honey
½ tablespoon dark rum
¼ cup very finely chopped roasted macadamia nuts

Heat oil in a saucepan and add garam masala. Stir to ensure even distribution and add green onion, plantain and salt.

Taro chips, red bean pâté and Fiji Islands dip

Stirring occasionally, cook for 5 minutes at a medium heat. Add chicken and cook for a further 5 minutes. Add honey and rum, and cook for a further minute. Serve hot, topped with roasted macadamia nuts on a canapé base.
Yield: 2 cups.

13

Samosas

DIPS & CHIPS

Delicious, crisp chips or French fries can be made from many starchy roots and fruits available from the tropics.

The chips should be fried in very hot oil, using a heavy deep saucepan. After cooking they should be lifted out, drained to remove surplus oil, and then placed on absorbent paper. Thick chips should be kept hot and served as soon as possible. Thin chips may be cooled and stored in a sealed container for future use.

It is also possible to oven bake thin or thick chips using hardly any oil, by coating them before cooking with herbs, spices or even garlic, They are delicious and very healthy.

Thin chips

Thin chips may be made from sweet potato, green bananas and plantains. Green bananas should be peeled like a potato using a paring knife. Rub a little oil on your hands to prevent staining.

Cut very thin slices of your selected vegetable with a sharp knife or use the slicing attachment on your food processor. Soak in a bowl of cold water for 30 minutes to draw out starch. Drain and dry on a cloth.

Fry in deep hot oil, drain, and dust with salt and pepper or chili powder just before serving. Do not add salt ahead of time as chips may go soft.

For oven baked chips, dry and toss in a tiny amount (maximum 2 teaspoons) olive oil and whatever flavoring you want — garlic, lemon grass and chili, spices or herbs, but no salt. Spread out on a greased baking tray and bake in a 275°F (140°C) oven until evenly golden and crisp. Cool and lightly salt just before serving.

Thick chips

Thick chips may be made from cooked taro, breadfruit, manioc (cassava) or sweet potato. Bake, boil or steam vegetables until soft but firm. Cut into pieces about 1–1½ inches (4 cm) long and ¼ inch (½ cm) thick. Fry in hot oil until crisp and golden brown. Dust with salt

Nimkies

Tiny savory cookies best served hot.

1 cup wholemeal flour
1 teaspoon baking powder
½ teaspoon salt
½ teaspoon ground cumin
¼ teaspoon turmeric
¼ teaspoon chili powder
2 tablespoons ghee or butter
3–4 tablespoons cold water
vegetable oil for deep frying

In a bowl, combine the first 6 ingredients. Rub in ghee or butter until crumbly. Sprinkle cold water over mixture and mix with a fork to make a stiff dough, similar to pastry. Roll dough very thinly, cut into small attractive shapes and leave to dry for 10 minutes.

In a deep pot heat oil to 375°F (190°C). Deep-fry, a few at a time, until puffy and golden. Drain well on paper towel. Serve hot.
Yield: 12–18 small cookies.

Note: If made in advance, nimkies may be reheated in a hot oven.

Samosas

pastry dough as for nimkies
¾ cup mashed potato
¼ cup cooked green vegetables
** (peas, chopped long beans**
** and celery)**
1 teaspoon curry powder
½ clove garlic, crushed
2 teaspoons lemon juice
salt and pepper
vegetable oil for deep frying

Prepare pastry dough and roll out very thinly. Cut into 3-inch (8-cm) squares. In a bowl combine all the remaining ingredients and mix well. Put spoonfuls of filling onto the center of the squares. Moisten edges with water, and fold dough over diagonally and press edges firmly to form triangles.

Deep fry samosas as for nimkies. Drain well and serve hot with a spicy chutney.
Yield: 4–6 samosas.

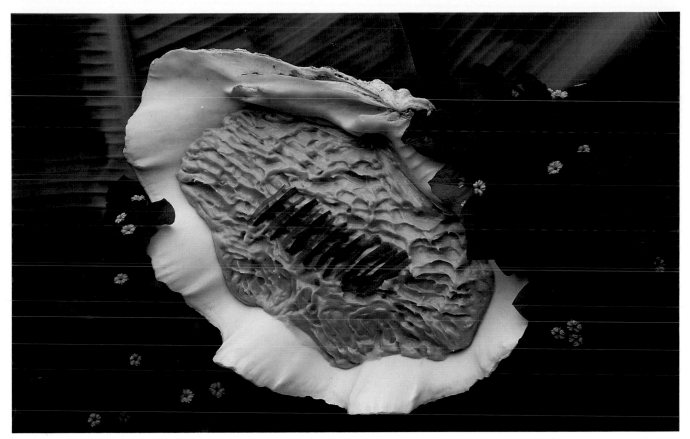

Guacamole

and pepper or chili powder. If none of these vegetables are available, use potato but do not pre-cook before frying.

If oven baking prepare as above, but before cooking coat in a tiny amount of oil and seasoning. Spread on a greased baking tray and bake in a hot 375°F (190°C) oven until evenly golden. Cool and lightly salt immediately before serving.

Tropical crudités

Strips of suitably contrasting vegetables such as zucchini, celery, carrot, daikon (white radish) and lightly blanched long beans and winged beans, together with strips of slightly under-ripe fresh pineapple, under-ripe papaya and mango, are an excellent and refreshing alternative to crackers, crisps or toasted squares. Crudités are excellent with guacamole (page 15), papaya and lime salsa (page 16) and red bean pâté (page 13).

Manioc (cassava) drops

Finely grate raw manioc and season with salt and pepper. Form into small round balls by gently rolling in your hands. Drop into hot oil and fry until golden brown.

Just before serving sprinkle with additional salt or a little curry powder, ground cumin, basil or any other desired spices or herbs.

Guacamole

A traditional Mexican dip.

1 large ripe avocado
1 medium tomato
¼ cup low fat or standard cream cheese
½ cup mayonnaise, light or standard
½ teaspoon chili powder
2 teaspoons finely chopped onion
1 small clove garlic, crushed
2 teaspoons lemon or lime juice
½ teaspoon ground cumin

Peel and mash avocado. Peel, de-seed and chop tomato. Combine all ingredients and mix well. Stand at

room temperature for 1 hour to develop flavor before serving. Serve with any variety of crackers, corn chips or crudités.
Yield: 2 cups.

Yogurt and cucumber dip (raita)

A delicious dip found in the cuisine of many tropical countries. It may also be served as a condiment with curries and pilau.

1 cup finely chopped cucumber
½ teaspoon salt
1 cup unsweetened natural yogurt
1 small clove garlic, crushed
1 teaspoon chopped fresh dill or ¼ teaspoon dried dill

Peel and chop cucumber. Place in a strainer, sprinkle with salt and allow to drain. Into the yogurt, mix the garlic and dill. Stir in the drained cucumber and adjust salt to taste. Refrigerate for 1 hour before serving.
Yield: 2 cups.

Papaya and lime salsa

A deceptively delicate salsa with a decided sting in the tail.

½ medium-sized papaya, slightly under-ripe
1 small fresh chili, de-seeded and finely chopped
1 small clove garlic, crushed
1 green or red pepper
2 limes
1 tablespoon honey
½ cup olive oil
1 teaspoon crushed green peppercorns
salt
cumin seeds

Mince or blend papaya, chili, garlic, pepper, juice of the limes and honey until finely chopped. Stir in olive oil and peppercorns and adjust seasoning. Chill before serving. Add a few cumin seeds as decoration.
Yield: 2 cups.

Eggplant dip

This dip is refreshing and easy to make. It provides an excellent contrast to the many heavy, creamy dips that are often used.

1¼ lb (500 g) eggplant (about 2 medium-sized fruit)
1 teaspoon coriander seeds
1 teaspoon black peppercorns
¾ cup fresh wholemeal breadcrumbs
¼ cup olive oil
¼ cup lemon juice
½ teaspoon salt
1 small onion, finely chopped
1 clove garlic, crushed
1 firm tomato
½ medium-sized green pepper
¼ cup chopped parsley

Bake the eggplant in a medium oven until soft, or microwave on high for 8 minutes. Cool and scoop the flesh out of the skins. Toast the coriander and black peppercorns in a pan over a medium heat, stirring all the time until the aroma has developed. Then coarsely grind in a peppermill. Blend the eggplant flesh, breadcrumbs, oil, salt and lemon juice until smooth and add finely chopped onion and crushed garlic.

De-seed tomato and pepper and chop into small cubes. Stir into dip and add parsley. Serve well chilled with baked or toasted bread fingers, biscuits or chips.
Yield: 1½ cups.

Fiji Islands dip

½ cup cooked white fish fillets
¼ cup freshly grated coconut
1 teaspoon lemon or lime juice
1 small clove garlic, crushed
½ cup sour cream or unsweetened natural yogurt
salt and pepper

Flake the cooked fish and mix in all remaining ingredients. Refrigerate for 2 hours to develop flavor before serving.

Note: Unsweetened desiccated coconut may be substituted for the fresh coconut. Use low fat yogurt for a very low calorie dip.
Yield: 1½ cups.

Coconut pesto

All varieties of basil grow prolifically all year round in the Pacific Island countries. Coconut combines with basil and garlic to make a different pesto which may be used as a spread or dip, or to enhance the flavor of Italian-type recipes.

1 cup grated coconut or ¾ cup desiccated coconut
¼ cup water
½ cup loosely packed basil leaves
2 cloves garlic
½ teaspoon salt
1 cup grated cheese (cheddar, Parmesan or similar)
¼ cup olive oil

Pound or blend grated coconut with basil, garlic, salt and water. Add cheese. Continue blending or mixing, at the same time slowly adding olive oil. Store in sterile jar, just covering the surface with oil. Refrigerate.
Yield: 1¼ cups.

COCKTAILS & SAUCES

Marinated fish (kokoda)— (pronounced kokonda)

A fish with fine but firm white flesh and not too many bones is best. The coconut sauce should be delicately flavored with onion, lemon, a little chili and possibly ginger or dill. Unless told, most people would not realise that this is raw fish. It can also be used for a more luxurious version using raw shellfish, such as lobster or prawns, but great care must be taken to ensure the freshness and cleanliness of the shellfish.

Kokoda is an excellent starter to a meal.

1½ lb (600 g) white fish
1 cup lime or lemon juice
1¼ cups coconut cream or lighter alternative (page 6)
¼ cup finely chopped onion
1 small chili, de-seeded and finely chopped
salt
grated carrot
tomato slices
lemon or lime slices
onion rings
chopped dill or chives

Remove the bones and skin from the fish and cut into ½-inch (1.5-cm) cubes. Place in a bowl, cover with lime or lemon juice and leave for about 2 hours. Strain fish and discard juice. Mix coconut cream with onion, chili and salt to taste, and pour over the fish. Garnish with carrot, tomato, lemon or lime slices, onion rings and chopped dill, or chives.
Yield: 6–8 portions.

Note: Do not cool to very low temperatures as this will make the coconut granular. For a more spicy flavor add 1 teaspoon of crushed green ginger root to the coconut cream.

Opposite above: Kokoda
Below: Watermelon and seafood mousse

Shrimp and avocado cocktail

2 tablespoons lemon juice
1½ cups ripe avocado, cubed
1½ cups cooked and shelled
   shrimps
1 tablespoon chopped chives or
   green onions (optional)
salt and pepper
¼ cup basic French dressing
   (page 28)

Sprinkle lemon juice over avocado.
Add shrimps and, if desired, chives
or green onions. Season to taste and
carefully place in small dishes on
lettuce leaves. Add French dressing.
Yield: 6 portions.

Kokoda with shrimps

1 lb (400 g) fish fillets, fresh or
   frozen (cod, halibut or white
   tuna)
1 cup lime or lemon juice
½ lb (200 g) cooked and shelled
   medium shrimps, fresh or
   frozen
2 cups coconut cream or light
   alternative (page 6)
½ medium-sized cucumber
1 teaspoon chopped fresh dill
salt

Cube the fish fillets and marinate in
lime or lemon juice as directed in
marinated fish (page 16). Strain.
Peel cucumber and dice. In a bowl
mix together the marinated fish,
shrimps (which should not be
chilled), coconut cream, cucumber
and dill. Season. Do not refrigerate
the mixture but serve in a chilled or
ice-surrounded dish.
Yield: 6–8 portions.

Seafood sauce

*A delightful and useful sauce that
can be used with any seafood combination. Try it with prawns, crab or
lobster along with some chopped
celery and lettuce.*

½ cup light or standard mayonnaise
   (page 28)
¼ cup tomato ketchup (page 90)
½ teaspoon Worcestershire sauce
1½ teaspoons lemon juice
dash cayenne pepper or chili
   powder
salt and pepper

Combine all ingredients. Serve with
any desired combination of seafood.
Yield: approx 1 cup.

Avocado with chilied tomato sauce

1 medium-sized tomato
3 teaspoons chili sauce
1 teaspoon sugar
2 tablespoons chopped green
   onion
½ cup light or standard
   mayonnaise (page 28)
salt
3 medium-sized avocados
2 tablespoons lemon juice

Peel, de-seed and finely chop tomato
and place in a bowl with chili sauce,
sugar, green onion and mayonnaise.
Add salt to taste. Stir well. Refrigerate for 2 hours to develop flavor. Cut
unpeeled avocados in half, remove
stones and sprinkle liberally with
lemon juice. Cover with plastic wrap
and refrigerate. Prior to serving fill
each cavity with sauce.
Yield: 6 portions.

Variation: Add crushed garlic to the
lemon juice and place about 1
tablespoon of caviar (lumpfish or
salmon) in each cavity. Decorate and
serve on a bed of chopped lettuce.

Exotic fruit cocktail

equal amounts of banana, guava
   papaya, pomelo (or similar),
   mangosteen or rambutan
   (canned if fresh not available)

Slice or cube fruit and chill for
several hours. Just before serving
add sweet vermouth dressing.

Sweet vermouth dressing

Combine ¼ cup sweet vermouth, 2
tablespoons green onion, ¼ teaspoon
sugar. Stir into 1 cup mayonnaise
(page 28.)

Watermelon and seafood mousse

1 tablespoon gelatine
¼ cup water
1½ cups cooked, flaked and
   shelled seafood (fresh or frozen
   or canned crab, shrimps or
   lobster)
1 cup cubed watermelon
¾ cup diced celery
½ cup light or standard
   mayonnaise (page 28)
2 tablespoons lemon juice
salt and pepper
½ cup whipped cream
lettuce, watercress or greens

Soften gelatine in water in a small
saucepan then heat until dissolved.
Cool. In a bowl combine it with
seafood, watermelon, celery, mayonnaise, lemon juice and seasoning.

Whip the cream and fold into the
mixture. Divide into six individual
molds or one large mold. Refrigerate
until set. Dip molds briefly into hot
water to release and set on a bed of
chopped lettuce, watercress or
greens such as rocket and sensopai.
Yield: 6 portions.

SOUPS

Good stock is the basis of all fine soups. It is worthwhile keeping a supply deep frozen. If home-made bone stock is not available, you can make quite a good substitute by simmering bouillon powder or cubes, or liquid stock concentrate, with the correct amount of water, and adding vegetables and herbs. Be very careful with the amount of salt added as bouillon cubes and powder tend to have a high salt content.

Many soups are equally good served hot or chilled. For hot weather menus we have included a number which are chilled.

The success of a chilled soup depends on serving it very cold. Just a few degrees above freezing point is best. To achieve this, soup bowls or cups must be thoroughly cooled before the meal, or arranged on a bed of crushed ice. Freeze a little of the soup mixture in an ice cube tray and put a cube or ball in each serving.

Cold soups need to be more highly seasoned than hot soups, as chilling dulls the sense of taste. Whilst hot, the soup should taste a little over-seasoned, but when cold it will be just right. Ensure that there is no surface fat as, when chilled, this will produce an unpleasant grainy texture. Remove any excess fat with kitchen paper.

Serve soups with colorful and tasty garnishes. These may vary from chopped crisp cucumber or thin slices of tomato, to toasted chopped macadamia nuts, toasted sesame seeds or croutons. Use cubed bread of different types and flavors to provide extra interest.

Coconut fish soup

Coconut fish soup

2 lb (800 g) fish heads and carcass
(cod, snapper or similar)
7 cups water
2 teaspoons salt
1 large onion, quartered
dash pepper
1 small chili, whole
1 tablespoon lemon juice
2 cups thick coconut cream or
lighter alternative (page 6)
lemon slices and chopped green
onions for garnish

Put the first six ingredients into a
large saucepan and bring slowly to
simmering point and maintain until
fish is soft. Skim periodically. Strain
off stock and adjust seasoning if
necessary. Stir in lemon juice and
coconut cream and heat thoroughly
but do not boil. Garnish each serving
with lemon slices and chopped green
onions.
Yield: 6 portions.

Herb-scented tomato soup

2 lb (800g) tomatoes
1½ tablespoons vegetable oil
1 clove garlic, crushed
1 small onion, chopped
1 teaspoon chopped fresh mint or
¼ teaspoon dried mint
½ teaspoon fresh chopped basil or
¼ teaspoon dried basil
1 teaspoon fresh chopped parsley
½ teaspoon chopped fresh
marjoram and oregano or ¼
teaspoon dried marjoram or
oregano
3 cups beef stock
2 teaspoons sugar
salt
2 tablespoons cornstarch
2 tablespoons water
6 tablespoons heavy cream, crème
fraîche or low fat sour cream
chopped chives or whole mint
leaves to garnish

Peel and chop tomatoes. Heat oil in
a large saucepan and sauté garlic
and onion until golden. Add tomatoes and chopped herbs. Stir well
and simmer for 5 minutes. Add beef
stock, sugar and salt. Cover and
simmer for 20 minutes.
Strain the mixture through a sieve
and measure. Add extra stock if

needed to make 6 servings. Mix
cornstarch and water to a smooth
paste and stir into soup. Gently
simmer. Serve hot or well chilled,
and garnish with a spoonful of heavy
or whipped cream, mixed with
chopped chives or mint leaves.
Yield: 6 portions.

Microwave note: This soup may be
made in a large casserole. Simmer
tomato-herb mixture on medium for
3 minutes then strain. After adding
stock etc., bring to the boil on high
then simmer for 10 minutes on
medium.

Shellfish soup

3 dozen small river kais, sea kai,
small clams, or oysters, or
sufficient shellfish to provide 2
cups of cooked flesh
2½ cups water
1 teaspoon salt
½ medium onion, chopped
2½ cups milk or tomato juice
dash Tabasco or chili sauce
4 tablespoons butter or margarine
4 tablespoons flour
4 teaspoons lemon juice
chopped chives or green onions
lemon slices and parsley for
garnish

Wash shellfish to remove sand.
Open up by putting in hot water and
cutting hinge muscle. Remove any
inedible parts and extract the flesh
from the shells. Reserve a few for
garnishing and put remainder into a
large saucepan. Add water, salt and
half the onion. Bring to simmering
point and cook until the flesh is just
tender (overcooking will toughen it).
Drain and reserve the stock. Put the
flesh into a blender and reduce to a
purée. Combine purée, milk and
Tabasco with stock.
In the saucepan melt butter or
margarine and gently sauté remaining onion, stir in the flour and cook
for 1 minute. Reduce heat and
slowly stir in the stock mixture.
Increase heat and bring to the boil,
stirring continuously. Reduce heat
and simmer for 5 minutes. Adjust
seasoning if necessary.
Just before serving, slowly stir in
lemon juice. Serve hot, garnished
with reserved shellfish, chives or
green onion, lemon slices and
parsley.
Yield: 6 portions.

Microwave note: Cook the first 6
ingredients in a large casserole on
high for 12 minutes, then on
medium for 10 minutes. Proceed
as directed, then reheat soup
thoroughly on medium, stirring
occasionally.

Shellfish soup

Opposite: Herb-scented tomato soup

Eggplant (aubergine) soup

Excellent for entertaining, served hot or cold. People who don't usually like eggplant will enjoy this.

1¼ lb (500g) eggplant
3 tablespoons lemon juice
1 large clove garlic, crushed
2 lean bacon rashers, chopped
2 tablespoons vegetable oil
1 medium onion, chopped
½ teaspoon ground coriander
6 cups chicken or vegetable stock
salt and freshly ground black
    pepper
1 tablespoon anchovy sauce
    (optional)
6 tablespoons yogurt for garnish
parsley or green coriander for
    garnish

Peel eggplant, cut into 1-inch (2.5-cm) cubes. Put in a bowl and stir in lemon juice and garlic, ensuring all pieces are covered. Refrigerate for about 3 hours.

Scatter the chopped bacon into a large cold saucepan, add oil and gently stir-fry until it begins to cook. Add onion and coriander and fry gently until golden. Add the egg-plant and cook for 5 minutes. Add stock, season with salt and pepper and simmer for 20–30 minutes.

Strain out some of the liquid and blend the remaining mixture until smooth. Return to saucepan and add extra stock, if needed, to make 6 servings. Add anchovy sauce, if desired, stir well and reheat or chill, including extra seasoning if soup is to be served chilled. Garnish with a spoonful of yogurt and chopped parsley, or coriander leaves.
Yield: 6 portions.

Leafy green soup

A delicious creamy soup using almost any variety of green leafy vegetables.

½ lb (200 g) green leafy vegetables
    (spinach, Chinese cabbage (pak
    choi), Swiss chard, watercress,
    lettuce, Japanese greens or taro
    leaves)
salt
4 tablespoons butter or margarine
1 small onion, chopped
1 clove garlic
¼ teaspoon curry powder
4 tablespoons flour
3 cups milk, standard or low fat
3 cups chicken or vegetable stock
½ teaspoon grated lemon rind
dash Tabasco sauce (optional)
salt and pepper
6 tablespoons coconut cream
    (optional)
chives or green onions, chopped

Wash thoroughly and coarsely chop green leaves. Cook in a large pot in a minimum of boiling, lightly salted water until just tender, about 5 minutes. Do not overcook, as color is important. However, if using taro leaves, these must be boiled for at least 10 minutes. Drain and purée.

In a large saucepan melt butter. Add onion, garlic and curry powder, and cook for 1 minute. Stir in flour and cook for 1 minute, then gradually add heated milk and stock. Add lemon rind and Tabasco sauce. Bring to the boil and simmer for 2–3 minutes. Stir in the purée of green vegetables. Add salt and pepper to taste.

Serve hot or well chilled. Garnish each serving with a spoonful of coconut cream and chopped chives or green onions.
Yield: 6 portions.

Microwave note: Put chopped leaves and onion in large casserole dish and add ¼ cup of water. Cover and cook on high for 4 minutes, stirring once. Set aside uncovered and undrained. Proceed with making soup base using another deep casserole dish. Purée undrained greens just before adding to the soup base.

Cucumber soup with yogurt

This refreshing soup is equally good served hot or cold. Originally from Balkan countries, the recipe has become popular throughout the South Pacific. It can be made with chicken or fish stock.

2 tablespoons vegetable oil
1 clove garlic, crushed
1 small onion, chopped
2 lb (800 g) green cucumbers,
    sliced
1 teaspoon salt
3 cups stock
2 tablespoons cornstarch
1½ cups natural unsweetened
    yogurt
2 tablespoons white wine
1 teaspoon chopped fresh dill
chopped chives, cucumber slices,
    for garnish

Heat the oil in a large saucepan and sauté the garlic and onion for 1 minute. Do not let them brown. Add cucumber and salt, and stir-fry for a few minutes. Stir in stock and boil for 5 minutes with lid off, to avoid discoloration of the cucumber. Cool and blend to a fine purée or rub through a sieve or strainer. Mix the cornstarch with the yogurt until smooth. Put into the saucepan and stir until boiling. Simmer for 1 minute, remove and cool.

Just before serving, combine thickened yogurt with cucumber mixture, wine and dill. For a cold soup, keep ingredients well chilled. Serve garnished with chopped chives and peeled cucumber slices.
Yield: 6 portions.

Note: This soup should be pale green in color. If necessary, add a little green food coloring or a table-spoon of spinach purée. The acid of the yogurt causes the natural green color to fade, and because of this we recommend adding yogurt at the last minute.

Microwave note: Put oil into 8-cup casserole. Cook on high for 1 minute. Add garlic and onion and cook on high for 1 minute. Stir in the cucumber, cover and cook on high for

6–7 minutes. Cool, blend and rub through strainer. Mix cornstarch with yogurt. Cook on high for 1 minute. Stir and return for 1–2 minutes. Just before serving combine all ingredients.

Dhal soup

Many kinds of dried split peas, or dhals, are used by Indian people in daily meals. Dhals are seasoned with onion, garlic and spices and served as soups, or thick purées, with rice, often accompanied by yogurt and fresh chutney. The dried peas are an excellent source of protein, minerals and some vitamins, and are highly recommended for vegetarian meals.

The following recipe may be varied by changing the type of dhal, the spices or including chopped vegetables.

1½ cups dhal (dried yellow split peas)
6 cups water, chicken or vegetable stock
3 cloves garlic, peeled
½ medium onion, chopped
1 medium chili, chopped (optional)
4 curry leaves (optional)
salt
2 teaspoons butter or ghee
2 cloves garlic, finely sliced
½ onion, finely chopped
½ teaspoon turmeric
½ teaspoon cumin seeds

Wash the dhal, add water and soak for 2–3 hours. Add 3 cloves garlic, ½ onion, chili, curry leaves and salt, and cook over medium heat until the dhal is very soft. Skim off the froth and discard. Add extra water or stock to make 6 cups. Blend dhal until very smooth. (This may not be necessary for soft dhals).

Heat the butter in a large saucepan, add garlic and second ½ onion and stir-fry until golden. Add remaining spices and stir over a medium heat for about 2 minutes. Stir in the dhal and simmer for about 10 minutes before serving.

Note: This soup is very good garnished with small toasted croutons, a spoonful of yogurt, or finely chopped fresh tomato.

Dhal soup

Microwave note: The soaked dhal may be cooked on high in a covered deep casserole until very soft — about 20 minutes, stirring 2 or 3 times. Cook the ghee, onion and spices in a small glass dish for 2 minutes on high; then add to the soup. For convenience use a thermometer probe to regulate the soup temperature to 170°F (77°C) for serving.

SALAD & DRESSINGS

A chilled salad is an ideal dish for the tropical menu. In many hot countries traditional salads are not served frequently because the familiar ingredients, such as lettuce, are not always available.

However there are a number of tropical green, leafy vegetables which have an excellent flavor when served raw, whilst others may be lightly blanched. These can be used to make new and different salads as compared with those made from Western vegetables.

The flavor of tropical salads may be enhanced by the inclusion of traditional Indian and Chinese spices in dressings.

It is a good idea to keep one or two basic dressings in bottles in the refrigerator. Different flavorings may then be added to suit the salad of the day.

It is very important to wash and inspect all raw salad vegetables very thoroughly. Dry in a wire basket or hang in a cloth bag before making your salad.

Tropical salads

Interesting salads can be made from a number of lightly blanched vegetable shoots and stems.

Many of the easily grown leafy vegetables like creeping or English spinach, Chinese cabbage (pak choi), water spinach (kangkong), red chicory, Japanese sensopai, mizuna, rocket and many others may be added to a mixed green salad.

Young taro or beet stems
Very carefully peel off the outer skin and cut the stalks into 4-inch (10-cm) lengths, tie in bundles, plunge into boiling water and cook rapidly for 2 minutes. Remove, cool and then shred with a sharp knife. Serve with lemon juice or any other type of dressing.

Pumpkin tops
Select the young tips of vines and prepare as for young taro or beet stems.

Bean sprouts
The sprouts of a number of beans and peas make delicious crisp salads. Serve plain or mixed with other greens.

Sweet potato
Scrub well and then steam or boil until soft. When cool, remove skin.

Taro
Peel first, then steam or boil until soft. Cube and use as for potato in potato salads.

Yam and breadfruit
Puncture with a skewer, then bake or steam in the skin, or peel and boil.

Cooking banana (plantain)
Boil or steam, then peel and slice.

Tasty rice salad

2 hard boiled eggs, chopped
2 tablespoons capers
3 cups cooked rice (use brown rice for more flavor and fiber)
½ cup light or standard mayonnaise (page 28)
½ teaspoon fennel or caraway seed
salt and freshly ground pepper
1 cup peeled and finely chopped cucumber
½ cup chopped parsley

In a bowl toss eggs, capers and rice. Moisten with mayonnaise. Season with fennel, salt and pepper. Refrigerate and before serving fold in the chopped cucumber and parsley.
Yield: 6 portions.

Mixed green salad

¼ lb (100 g) Chinese cabbage (pak choi) leaves and stalks, shredded
¼ lb (100 g) spinach leaves
¼ lb (100 g) watercress
¼ lb (100 g) other greens (sweet potato vine tops, edible fern tips or Japanese greens) or 2 cups of each of the above, prepared
1 cup bean or pea sprouts
½ cup chopped parsley, green onion or mixed fresh herbs

Wash leaves well, shake dry and put into a plastic bag in the refrigerator to crisp. Shred the cabbage and tear the spinach leaves. Take the leaves off the cress and discard the tough stems.

Use the tips of the sweet potato vine, including young whole leaves. Lightly blanch fern tips. Tear the Japanese green leaves. Add sprouts and herbs and toss with a well-flavored dressing.
Yield: 8–10 portions.

Note: Any other suitable leaves may be used in roughly the same proportions. It is important to see that the stronger-flavored kinds are combined with those of milder flavor.

Lemon eggplant salad

1½ lb (600 g) eggplant
2½ cups water
½ cup salad oil
½ teaspoon coriander seeds
1 teaspoon salt
½ cup lemon juice or white wine vinegar
¼ cup fresh herbs (basil, parsley, tarragon) or 3 teaspoons dried mixed herbs
1 bay leaf
½ cup currants or sultanas
lemon slices and chopped parsley for garnish

Lemon eggplant salad

Peel and dice eggplant into ½-inch (1.5-cm) cubes. Place water, salad oil, coriander, salt, lemon juice, fresh herbs and bay leaf in a saucepan. Bring to the boil, add eggplant and simmer until just tender but firm. Remove eggplant and reduce liquid by half through boiling. Strain.

Add currants or sultanas to liquid and simmer for 5 more minutes. Pour over cooked eggplant and chill. Serve with lemon slices and chopped parsley.
Yield: 6 portions.

Pak choi cabbage and carrot salad

Any type of cabbage may be used but the Chinese cabbage does give greater flavor and color.

1½ cups finely shredded pak choi
1½ cups finely grated carrot
1 cup blue cheese dressing
   (page 28) or coconut cream

Toss shredded cabbage and grated raw carrot together. Place half cup of salad on each plate with 2 tablespoons of blue cheese dressing, coconut cream or light alternative dressing on top.
Yield: 6 portions.

Vegetable raita

A tangy yogurt salad traditionally served with curries or pilau.

1 cup cubed cucumber
½ teaspoon salt
2 cups cooked and cubed potato
½ small onion, finely chopped
2 medium tomatoes, finely
   chopped
2 cups natural unsweetened
   yogurt
¼ teaspoon cumin seeds
salt

Place cucumber in a strainer and sprinkle with salt. Let stand to drain off any juice. In a bowl mix cucumber, potato, onion and tomatoes with yogurt. Add cumin seeds and season with salt if desired. Serve immediately.
Yield: 6 portions.

Variation: Substitute cooked taro, manioc or sweet potato for potato. Substitute 2 tablespoons chopped green onions for onion. Green peppers or celery may be added or used instead of cucumber. Add 2 tablespoons fresh parsley, mint or coriander.

Tahitian fish salad

Tahitian fish salad

An excellent dieters' meal if low calorie dressing is used.

1 lb (400 g) white fish
1 teaspoon salt
½ cup lemon juice
½ small onion, chopped
1 medium carrot, grated
1 medium cucumber, cubed
1 green pepper, sliced
2 cups shredded Chinese (pak choi) or English cabbage
2–3 tomatoes, diced
½ cup French dressing, mayonnaise, coconut cream or lighter alternatives (page 28)

Cut the fish into ½-inch (1.5-cm) cubes and put into a bowl. Sprinkle with salt and stir well. Cover with lemon juice and leave for 2 hours. Strain and discard juice. Chill.

Combine the fish with the prepared vegetables. Just before serving toss in your choice of dressing.

Yield: 6 portions.

Shrimp rice salad

24 shrimps or 1 lb (400g) small shrimps
2 bacon rashers
4 cups cooked rice
1 cup cubed celery or cucumber
¼ cup grated coconut
½ lb (200 g) segments fresh citrus fruit (tangelo, pomelo, orange, mandarin or pink grapefruit)
½ cup sour cream, low fat or standard
2 teaspoons lemon juice
salt
watercress for garnish

Cut large shrimps into thirds, but leave small shrimps whole. Finely chop bacon and fry until golden. Mix shrimps, rice, celery, bacon, coconut and citrus segments together. Combine the sour cream and lemon juice and fork into the mixture, adding salt to taste. Chill and serve on a bed of watercress.

Yield: 6 portions.

Sunset salad

An aptly named salad because of its delectable color.

1½ lb (600 g) eggplant
2 tablespoons vegetable oil

Sauce:
1 large onion, finely chopped
1 large clove garlic, crushed
¼ cup olive oil
1½ tablespoons tomato paste
1 cup tomato juice
1½ tablespoons chopped anchovies
1 tablespoon red wine vinegar
1 teaspoon sugar
1 teaspoon salt
½ cup finely chopped fresh parsley or 2 tablespoons parsley, dried
1 cup finely chopped celery
chopped parsley, black olives, capers and wholemeal bread

Peel and cut eggplant into 1-inch (2.5-cm) cubes. Heat vegetable oil in a heavy saucepan and then sauté the eggplant until soft but still firm. Drain well and place on absorbent paper until the sauce is ready.
Sauce: Sauté the onion and garlic in oil in a heavy saucepan until soft. Stir in tomato paste and tomato juice. Add anchovies, vinegar, sugar, salt and parsley. Simmer 5–10 minutes. Blanch celery in boiling water for 2 minutes. Drain and stir celery and eggplant into sauce.

Serve well chilled as an appetizer, garnished with freshly chopped parsley, black olives and capers on thick slices of buttered, toasted wholemeal or rye bread.

Yield: 6 portions.

Variation: For a more substantial dish, fold in 2 cups of cold flaked tuna.

Indian spiced vegetable salad

This dish provides a delicious first course to a meal and is very suitable for a vegetarian menu.

10 oz (250 g) okra, fresh or frozen, or zucchini
2 tablespoons tamarind pulp or 1½ tablespoons lemon juice
1 cup water
3 tablespoons vegetable oil
½ tablespoon mustard seed
½ tablespoon cumin seed
¼ teaspoon chili powder or 1 small chili, de-seeded
1 tablespoon mild or hot curry powder, according to taste
2 bay leaves
1 clove garlic, crushed
1 medium onion, finely chopped
1 large potato, peeled and diced
salt
2 cups cooked rice
lettuce
natural unsweetened yogurt
chopped parsley and coriander
1–2 tomatoes

Cut okra into ½-inch (1.5-cm) pieces, or slice zucchini. Mix tamarind pulp with the water. In a large saucepan, heat oil and sauté the spices and bay leaves for 1 minute. Add garlic and onion and stir-fry for 3 minutes. Add okra and potato and sauté for 5 minutes. Strain tamarind water onto vegetables and simmer until potato is cooked (about 5 minutes). Add salt if desired. Remove bay leaves. Gently stir in rice with a fork.

Transfer mixture to a bowl and refrigerate until serving time. Serve chilled on lettuce. Garnish with yogurt, chopped herbs and tomato wedges.
Yield: 6 portions.

Spiced sweet potato and banana salad

1 lb (400 g) sweet potato, cooked
4 ripe bananas
¼ cup lemon juice
2 tablespoons vegetable oil
2 teaspoons curry powder
2 cloves garlic, crushed
½ cup standard or light mayonnaise (page 28)
¼ cup chopped green onions
chopped parsley or coriander

Cut cooked sweet potato into 1-inch (2.5-cm) cubes. Slice bananas and marinate in lemon juice. Heat oil in saucepan. Sauté curry powder and garlic. Cool and mix with mayonnaise to form curry dressing.

Combine banana and sweet potato. Fold in dressing and chopped green onions. Garnish with chopped parsley or coriander.
Yield: 6–8 portions.

SALAD DRESSINGS

Quick dressings

A whole range of thick or thin, rich or low calorie dressings can be made very quickly and easily using a blender.

Standard dressing:

1 part acid — vinegar, or freshly squeezed lemon or lime juice
3 parts oil — a good quality oil such as olive, corn or sunflower.

Remember that inferior vinegar or oil will ruin the flavor of the dressing. One secret for a special dressing is to combine oils with different flavors and bases such as peanut or walnut oil. Try keeping olive oil, for example, in which are marinaded four cloves of garlic and one whole chili per liter of oil.

To the basic recipe, you can add a range of seasonings that will match other food being served — and the content of the salad. For creaminess, add one or two egg yolks.

To prepare, always follow this routine: In a blender, first place the acid, all seasonings, and egg yolks if required. Blend quickly for about 5 seconds. Add oil gradually and blend for about 10 seconds. Taste and adjust seasoning. The dressing is now ready and can be bottled, provided it is kept in a cool place.

It is a good idea to have different dressings available. Unfortunately, those described above, and mayonnaise, have a lot of oil, adding perhaps unwanted calories. There is no need to have rich dressings. Salads can be tossed in a flavored vinegar (page 91).

Salad dressings clockwise top left: Tomato, blue cheese, banana radish, curry, papaya seed.

27

In many recipes the oil content may be halved and lemon juice or vinegar adjusted for flavor. Do not use a basic vinegar as the acidity can overwhelm the food it is accompanying. In vinaigrette-type dressings, less oil may be distributed through the dressing by including a little gelatine. Try our low calorie vinaigrette which gives the flavor of olive oil without the calories.

Mayonnaise

1 egg yolk
½ teaspoon salt
½ teaspoon dry mustard
1 cup olive or good quality oil
1–2 tablespoons good quality vinegar or lemon juice

Beat egg yolk with salt and mustard. Add oil drip by drip, beating continuously until mayonnaise thickens, then add remaining oil. When thick, beat in vinegar. Refrigerate.
Yield: approx 1 cup.

Low calorie mayonnaise

½ cup mayonnaise
½ cup natural unsweetened, low fat yogurt
¼ teaspoon crushed garlic
1 egg white, stiffly beaten
salt

Fold yogurt into mayonnaise. Season with salt and garlic. Before serving, fold in beaten egg white.
Yield: 1½ cups.

Basic vinaigrette (French) dressing

1 small clove garlic
1 teaspoon salt
freshly ground black pepper
1 teaspoon sugar
¼ cup lemon juice or white wine vinegar
¾ cup good quality salad oil

Crush garlic in salt, add black pepper and sugar. Beat in lemon juice or wine vinegar and then add salad oil. Store in a bottle or jar and shake well before using. Refrigerate.
Yield: 1 cup.

Variations:
French herb dressing
Just before serving, add 1 tablespoon of finely chopped herbs or 1 teaspoon of dried herbs to every ½ cup of French dressing.

Curry dressing
Add 1 teaspoon of curry powder to 1 cup of French dressing.

Blue cheese dressing
Add 2 oz (50 g) blue cheese to 1 cup of French dressing. Mash cheese with a fork and beat into dressing. (Alternatively, put all ingredients in a blender and mix until smooth).

Tomato dressing
Use 2 tablespoons of tomato purée and 2 tablespoons of lemon juice in the basic French dressing recipe in place of ¼ cup lemon juice.

Low calorie vinaigrette dressing

1 teaspoon gelatine
1 tablespoon cold water
½ cup boiling water
¼ cup white wine vinegar or lemon juice
2 tablespoons olive oil
salt and freshly ground black pepper
1 clove garlic, crushed
1 olive (optional)

Mix gelatine with cold water and melt in boiling water. Add to other ingredients and shake well. Cool and refrigerate. If desired, add olive for extra flavor. Shake before serving.
Yield: 1 cup.

Banana radish dressing

Excellent dressing to perk up coleslaw.

2 ripe bananas
2 tablespoons peeled and finely grated white radish (daikon)
1 tablespoon lemon juice
salt
1 teaspoon sugar
dash Worcestershire sauce

Mash bananas to yield about 1 cup. Add a little of the lemon juice to avoid discoloration. Combine all

ingredients and blend until smooth. Refrigerate and pour over coleslaw just before serving.
Yield: 1½ cups.

Sesame oil dressing

Excellent on rice, bean sprouts.

½ cup sesame oil
½ cup salad oil
½ cup lemon juice
3 teaspoons mild soy sauce
1 teaspoon prepared mustard
dash pepper

Blend or beat all ingredients thoroughly. Put into a jar with a tight-fitting lid and shake vigorously until thoroughly mixed. Keeps very well.
Yield: 1½ cups.

Papaya seed dressing

An exotic creamy dressing using the peppery seeds of fresh papaya.

1 tablespoon fresh papaya seeds
1 cup corn oil
½ cup cider vinegar
2 tablespoons finely chopped onion
1 tablespoon sugar
½ teaspoon dry mustard
salt

Blend all ingredients until a smooth creamy dressing is achieved. Alternatively, mash papaya seeds on a plate, then put all ingredients into a jar with a tight-fitting lid and shake vigorously until creamy.

Serve as the dressing for a papaya-banana-apple salad or as a sauce for seafood cocktails. Refrigerate.
Yield: 2 cups.

Coconut cream dressing

1 cup thick coconut cream
¼ cup lemon juice
salt
1 teaspoon grated onion
½ teaspoon chopped chili

Combine all ingredients and serve fresh. Alternatively, the dressing can be left to ferment for a few days at room temperature. During this time it develops a stronger acid flavor.
Yield: 1½ cups.

BRUNCH & SAVORY CRÊPES

Chicken pilau

In this chapter we suggest you try a variety of light and sometimes spicy recipes. Curries and pilaus add variety and color to a meal. Make sure you serve these with a fresh flavored chutney or pickle (pages 90–92).

Chicken or lamb pilau

1 clove garlic, crushed
1 small onion, finely chopped
2 tablespoons vegetable oil
3 whole cloves
6 whole peppercorns, green or red
1 x 1½-inch (4-cm) cinnamon stick
2 cardamom pods
1 teaspoon turmeric
1½ cups raw, long grain rice
3 cups chicken stock or water
¼ cup raisins
½ teaspoon salt
1–2 cups chopped, half-cooked, chicken or lamb
1 tablespoon butter
¼ cup almond halves, blanched or chopped macadamias

In a large cast iron casserole or saucepan, sauté garlic and onion in the vegetable oil. Bruise cloves, peppercorns, cinnamon and cardamom with a rolling pin or wooden spoon. Add to saucepan. Add turmeric and cook gently for 3–4 minutes. Add rice and cook, stirring constantly, for about 5 minutes. Add the stock and salt, and bring to the boil. Cook for 5 minutes, then stir in the chopped chicken or lamb. Cover tightly and put saucepan/casserole in the oven at 200°F (100°C) for 20 minutes to steam.

Heat the butter in a pan and fry the nuts until golden. Add the raisins and stir-fry until plump. Serve the pilau in a colorful dish, garnished with nuts and raisins.
Yield: 6 portions.

29

Seafood spinach quiche

¾ cup cooked and chopped taro
   leaves, spinach, or Swiss chard
9-inch (23-cm) unbaked short
   pastry shell (page 76)
1 cup shrimp, crabmeat or your
   favorite seafood combination
1 tablespoon finely chopped onion
½ cup grated cheese (Cheddar or
   Swiss)
2 tablespoons grated Parmesan
   cheese
salt and dash cayenne pepper
2 eggs
¾ cup milk, standard or low fat
Note: If using taro leaves, boil for
at least 10 minutes.

Spread the well-drained, cooked and
chopped leaves over the pastry base.
Add well-drained seafood. Sprinkle
onion and cheese on top. Season to
taste. Beat eggs and milk together
and carefully pour over ingredients
in shell. Bake immediately in a
425°F (220°C) oven for 10 minutes
then reduce heat to 350°F (175°C)
and bake for a further 25 minutes
until the center is set.
Yield: 6 portions.

Coconut egg curry

Coconut egg curry

*Variations on this recipe are to be
found around the world of tropical
islands. Sometimes when hen's eggs
are not available those of seabirds
are used, introducing completely
different flavors.*

1 whole fresh coconut or ¾ cup
   desiccated coconut soaked in
   ½ cup of water
1 tablespoon lemon juice
4 medium onions, thinly sliced
3 tablespoons ghee, butter or oil
1 teaspoon turmeric
1 teaspoon ground coriander
½ teaspoon chili powder
salt
6 eggs, hardboiled
6 cups cooked long-grained rice

Crack the coconut (page 6) and
reserve the liquid. Grate the flesh,
then mix with lemon juice and set
aside. Crush about ¼ cup of onions
with a wooden spoon. In a saucepan
heat ghee and fry the onion. Add
turmeric, coriander and chili powder
and stir-fry for 1 minute. Stir in the
grated coconut and cook for 5
minutes. Add remaining onions and

reserved coconut liquid. Simmer
until the onions are tender, about 10
minutes. Add salt to taste. Slice or
quarter the eggs and place in a
heated serving bowl, then cover with
the hot sauce. Keep hot for 10
minutes before serving, to allow
flavor to penetrate. Serve with rice.
Yield: 6 portions.

Vegetable shrimp omelet with soy sauce broth

8 eggs
½ cup water
1 cup cooked shrimps
4 tablespoons vegetable oil
½ lb (200 g) fresh bean sprouts,
   drained
1 medium green pepper, finely
   chopped
4 green onions, finely chopped
salt and pepper

In a large bowl, beat the eggs and
water together. Add the shrimps. In
a heavy frypan or wok, heat the oil
and stir-fry the bean sprouts, pepper
and green onions for 3 minutes. Lift
out with a slotted spoon and add to
the egg mixture. Season with salt
and pepper. Pour about one-sixth of
the mixture at a time into the hot
lightly oiled frypan. Tilt the pan to
spread the mixture evenly and cook
until it is lightly brown underneath
and the surface is dry. Fold the
omelet in half and cook half a
minute more. Serve immediately
with the soy sauce broth.
Yield: 6 portions.

Note: Shredded cooked ham or pork
may be used instead of shrimps.

Soy sauce broth

¼ cup mild soy sauce
2 tablespoons sugar
2 tablespoons white vinegar
1 cup chicken stock

Put all ingredients into a saucepan
and bring to the boil. Reduce heat to
very low and allow to slowly simmer
while making the omelet.
Yield: 1½ cups.

Opposite: Seafood spinach quiche

Sensopai and taro leaf cheese soufflé

Coconut cream fish soufflé

**1 cup thick coconut cream or
  lighter alternative (page 6)**
3 tablespoons flour
1 teaspoon salt
¼ cup finely chopped onion
2 teaspoons lemon juice
dash chili sauce
1 cup cooked fish or shellfish
4 eggs

Prepare coconut cream (page 6). In a
saucepan blend flour and coconut
cream. Stir in salt and onion. Place
over medium heat and bring to
boiling point, stirring constantly.
Reduce heat and simmer for 3
minutes. Add lemon juice and chili
sauce. Cool, then add cooked fish or
shellfish.

Separate eggs. Beat egg whites
until stiff but not dry. Beat yolks
until thick and creamy and combine
with sauce. Fold in egg whites until
fairly evenly mixed. Spoon into a
lightly greased soufflé dish. Bake at
375°F (190°C) for 30–35 minutes.
Serve immediately.
Yield: 4 portions.

SAVORY CREPES

The versatility of crêpes earns them
special attention. Simple to make
they can be filled with either a sweet
or savory filling and used for
entrées, main courses or desserts.
Spicy or fruity tropical fillings make
crêpes a quick and interesting meal
or addition to a menu.

Crêpes may be produced ahead of
time, cooled, and then stacked with
greaseproof paper between layers.
Or they may be placed in a plastic
bag and refrigerated for up to 48
hours, or even frozen for 3–4 weeks.
A great time saver when entertaining.

Basic crêpes

1 cup flour
pinch of salt
3 eggs
2 tablespoons butter, melted
1½ cups milk, standard or low fat

Stir flour and salt together. Beat
eggs into the flour mixture, one at a

Sensopai and taro leaf cheese soufflé

*Any green leaf vegetables can be used
for this recipe. Make sure they are
not too bland as its secret lies in a
blending of flavors. Taro leaves must
be cooked for at least 10 minutes.*

3 tablespoons butter or margarine
3 tablespoons flour
1 teaspoon salt
1 teaspoon dry mustard
1 cup milk, standard or low fat
½ cup grated Cheddar cheese
**½ cup cooked, well mashed
  sensopai and taro leaves, in
  equal quantities**
4 eggs

In a large saucepan, make a basic
white sauce (method page 10) using
the first 5 ingredients. Remove from
the heat and stir in cheese and
green leaves. Set aside.

Separate eggs. Beat egg whites
until stiff. Beat egg yolks until thick
and creamy and blend into sauce.
Gently fold the beaten egg whites
into the sauce until fairly evenly
mixed. Spoon into lightly greased
6-cup soufflé or straight-sided dish.
Bake in a pre-heated 375°F (190°C)
oven for 30–35 minutes. Do not open
oven door while baking. The soufflé
will have a golden brown, puffed-up
crown and a deep crack around the
edge when done. Serve immediately.
Yield: 4 portions.

Note: Omit sensopai and replace
with 1 cup spinach or taro leaves.
Some cooks prefer to set the dish in
a shallow pan of hot water during
baking.

time, beating well after each addition. Melt butter, blend with milk and slowly beat into the flour mixture. Leave to stand for 2 hours. Lightly oil a very hot frypan (cast iron is best) for large pancakes or a 5-inch (12-cm) one for smaller pancakes. Pour ¼ cup of batter into the large pan or 2 tablespoons into the smaller one. Tilt pan around until the batter is evenly distributed and ceases to run. When it is dry on top with fine bubbles, flip it over with the help of a spatula or fish slice. Cook for 1 minute more. Remove to wire rack to keep warm. Stack succeeding crêpes on top. Cover with wax paper and clean towel and heat in oven at 300°F (150°C) for 10 minutes.
Yield: 12 large or 24 small crêpes.

Smoked gamefish crêpes

Although any seafood can be used as a filling , the range of wonderful smoked fish available makes this much more exciting. Try smoked gamefish — marlin, swordfish, albacore, tuna and shark.

6 crêpes
2 cups seafood sauce (page 18)
1½ cups boneless chopped mixed smoked gamefish
chopped parsley or dill for garnish

Blend seafood sauce with chopped smoked fish, fill and roll crêpes and garnish with chopped parsley. Serve lightly chilled.
Yield: 6 portions.

Basic crêpes filled with seafood

Tropical ratatouille crêpes

6 crêpes
1 tablespoon peanut or vegetable oil
1 teaspoon ground coriander
1 teaspoon ground allspice
1 clove garlic, crushed
1 large onion, chopped
3 okra, sliced
3 tomatoes, skinned and chopped
1 large kumara, cooked and cubed
1 red pepper, sliced
1 chili, de-seeded and finely chopped
1 cup diced fresh pineapple
1 cup unsweetened orange juice
1 tablespoon raw sugar
salt
finely chopped parsley for garnish

Heat oil in saucepan. Add spices and garlic and cook for 1 minute. Add chopped onion and okra, and stir-fry for 3 minutes. Add remaining vegetables, pineapple, orange juice and sugar, and cook until the juice has almost evaporated, about 10 minutes. Adjust seasoning. Warm crêpes, fill with mixture and roll. Serve hot, garnished with finely chopped parsley.
Yield: 6 portions.

Chicken, mango and lime crêpes

6 crêpes
1 tablespoon butter, margarine or vegetable oil
2 cups cooked, boned finely diced chicken
1 cup fresh chopped mango
2 teaspoons fresh lime juice
1 teaspoon chili sauce
salt
6 slices fresh lime for garnish

Heat butter in saucepan and add chicken and mango. Cook for 2 minutes. Add lime juice, chili sauce and salt and cook a further 2 minutes. Warm crêpes, fill with mixture and roll. Serve hot with a twist of lime for garnish.
Yield: 6 portions.

33

FISH

F ish abound in the waters of the Pacific Islands. From the colorful and sweet-fleshed reef fish to the stronger flesh of the gamefish; from the delicate mangrove crabs to the rich texture of the crayfish, they present a splendid array and challenge for the inventive cook.

During the last 20 years, new fishing techniques have brought a wonderful selection of deep sea tropical fish into our markets. Amongst the best are the o'pakpaka, onaga, uhui and lehi. These firm-fleshed, flavorful fish are exported all over the world.

In this section we indicate the most widely available tropical fish, but these can be substituted with suitable temperate water types.

When buying fresh fish, always remember that the eyes must be bright and full, the flesh firm and the gills pink to reddish in color.

Fish poisoning

Fish poisoning may occur at different times throughout the tropics. It tends to be more prevalent in the hot seasons when some kinds of fish, which inhabit shallower waters, feed off toxic algae.

The incidence of poisoned fish varies and many places are quite free from it. Certain types of fish are more likely to be infected than others so it is important to seek local knowledge concerning the most reliable fish to eat at different times of the year. In general, deep sea fish are the safest to eat, particularly in the hot seasons.

Fish poisoning is seldom fatal, but does cause illness and uncomfortable after-effects. Like other forms of food poisoning, it can often be avoided through careful selection of the food eaten.

Unfortunately, to date, no reliable way of detecting poison in fish has been found.

Game fish

A number of game fish are highly prized for the flavor and texture of their flesh. Amongst the best found in tropical waters are the yellow fin tuna (prized as Japanese sashimi), mako shark, mahi mahi and sword-fish, although the latter is less common.

All game fish have firm flesh with a fairly high oil content. The flesh is best cut into fairly thick steaks for grilling, poaching and baking. Care should be taken to cook at a medium temperature for just long enough for the flesh to become firm and white. Overcooking makes the fish hard and tasteless. Game fish are excellent smoked.

Coconut creamed fish

1½ lb (600 g) fish fillets, frozen or fresh (bluefish, sole, cod)
½ cup seasoned flour
½ cup vegetable oil
2 cups coconut cream, or lighter alternative
2 tablespoons finely chopped onion
1 teaspoon salt
1 small chili, chopped (optional)
1 tablespoon cornstarch
2 medium tomatoes, sliced, or ½ cup cooked shrimps
lemon wedges
dill or parsley for garnish

Cut fish fillets into serving pieces. Dredge each piece in seasoned flour. Heat oil in frypan and fry fish until golden on each side. Transfer to a large casserole.

In a saucepan, put the coconut cream, onion, salt, chili, if desired, and cornstarch. Stir well then place over medium heat and bring to nearly boiling, stirring all the time. Do not boil, but keep at simmering point for 3 minutes. Pour over fish, top with tomato or shrimps and cover. Bake at 300°F (150°C) for about 20 minutes. Serve with lemon wedges and parsley or dill for garnish.
Yield: 6 portions.

Coconut creamed fish

Microwave note: Cook sauce on medium for 4 minutes. Add fish to casserole, cover and cook on high for 4 minutes, then on medium for 2 minutes. Stand for 5 minutes. Casserole may also be made well in advance. Undercook slightly as the fish will finish cooking during the reheating time.

Spiced fried fish

2 lb (800 g) fish fillets, frozen or
   fresh (cod, snapper or perch)
½ cup milk, standard or low fat
½ cup flour
1 teaspoon salt
2 teaspoons curry powder, or to
   your taste
¼ cup vegetable oil
1½ cups coconut cream, or lighter
   alternative (page 6)
lemon wedges for garnish

Cut fillets into servings, dip in milk,
and then in flour mixed with curry
powder and salt. In a heavy, large
frypan, heat the oil and fry the fish
on both sides until golden and it
flakes easily. Serve with coconut
cream on the side or, if you prefer,
cover the fish with coconut cream
and bake at 300°F (150°C) for 15
minutes. Serve with lemon wedges,
rice and a salad.
Yield: 6 portions.

Microwave note: Cook in the
microwave on medium for 8 minutes. Stand for 5 minutes.

Fish in green shirt

1½ lb (600 g) fish fillets, fresh or
   frozen (salmon, snapper or cod)
12 large rourou (taro) or chard
   leaves
1 large onion, chopped
salt
2 cups coconut cream or lighter
   alternative (page 6)
2 medium tomatoes

Cut fillets into 6 serving pieces.
Rinse taro leaves and remove stems.
To make leaves pliable, slice off half
the main rib or back of leaf, then
soak in hot water for a few minutes.
For individual parcels, arrange two
leaves well overlapped with top side
up. Place a fish fillet in middle,
sprinkle with chopped onion and
salt.

   Hold the leaf parcel cupped in one
hand and add a little coconut cream.
Then fold over leaves to close the
parcel and secure with a toothpick
or tie with white thread. Place all 6
parcels in a shallow casserole dish
and pour over remaining coconut

cream. Cut tomatoes in thick slices
and place on top. Cover and bake at
350°F (180°C) for 30–40 minutes
until the parcels are tender. Serve
hot.
Yield: 6 portions.

Microwave note: Delicious when
cooked on medium for 13 minutes.
Stir and spoon cream over parcels
midway through the cooking time.
Let stand for 5 minutes then test for
texture. Additional time may be
needed depending on the thickness
of parcels, or if closely packed and
layered in the casserole.

Fish curry

2 tablespoons vegetable oil, butter
   or margarine
1 medium onion, finely chopped
1 clove garlic, crushed
1 tablespoon curry powder, or to
   your taste
1 tablespoon tomato paste
3 medium tomatoes, peeled and
   chopped, or ¾ cup canned
   tomatoes, drained (reserve liquid)
2 tablespoons lemon juice
salt
1½ lb (600 g) fish fillets (best are
   those with strong flavors such
   as snapper, tuna, albacore and
   other gamefish)

In a deep frypan, sauté onion and
garlic in oil. Stir in curry powder,
reduce heat and cook for 3 minutes.
Stir in tomato paste and tomatoes,
and cook over a medium heat,
stirring well.

   If necessary, add some reserved
tomato liquid or water to thin sauce.
Stir in lemon juice and season with
salt if desired. Cut fish into 2-inch
(5-cm) pieces and add to sauce.
Simmer gently until fish is cooked
— about 15 minutes. Serve hot.
Yield: 6 portions.

Microwave note: Put oil, butter or
margarine in a large casserole and
cook on high for 30 seconds. Add
onion, garlic and curry powder, stir
well and cook on high for 2 minutes.
Stir in tomatoes, tomato paste,
lemon juice and salt. Cover and cook
on medium for 2–3 minutes, stirring
twice. Add fish pieces to this sauce,

cover and cook on high for 5 minutes.
Stand for 5 minutes.

Baked ginger fish

2-3 lb (800 g–1.2 kg) whole fish,
   fresh or frozen (snapper,
   grouper, ling or cod)
1 lemon
2 tablespoons vegetable oil
¼ cup soy sauce
¼ cup corn oil
¾ cup white wine or white grape
   juice
1 clove garlic, crushed
2 teaspoons grated fresh ginger
   root
2 teaspoons sugar
parsley, coriander or slivered
   ginger root for garnish

For an attractive serving effect,
choose a whole fish with head and
tail intact. If necessary, remove
scales, then rinse and dry fish well.
Cut lemon in half and squeeze,
rubbing juice into fish, inside and
out. Refrigerate for about an hour,
then rub with vegetable oil and
place in a shallow baking dish.

   In a blender, mix thoroughly soy
sauce, corn oil, white wine, garlic
and ginger. Pour over fish. Bake at
350°F (180°C) for about 40 minutes,
until the fish flakes easily and juices
are opaque. Baste with broth
frequently.

   Just before serving, sprinkle fish
with sugar and place under broiler
until sugar melts and it forms a
glaze.

   Serve on a wooden platter, garnish
with parsley, coriander or slivered
ginger. The pan broth may be served
alongside.
Yield: 6 portions.

Note: This dish can also be made
with fish fillets or steaks. Place in
casserole and proceed as above.

Microwave note: If fish is too long
to fit easily into the microwave
without touching the sides, then cut
off head and tail and proceed as
directed. The cooking time on high
will be 6–7 minutes per pound (400 g).

Opposite above: Spiced fried fish
Below: Baked ginger fish

Barbecued mako shark with fruit and peanut sauce

6 shark steaks of matching size
   (retain central bones but
   remove skin)
½ cup peanut oil
2 tablespoons lemon juice
1 tablespoon finely chopped fresh
   ginger root
1 teaspoon freshly ground black
   pepper
salt
8 oz (200 g) peanuts, shelled,
   unsalted, roasted
2 tablespoons peanut or vegetable
   oil
1 medium onion, finely chopped
1 clove garlic, crushed
2 green chilis, de-seeded and
   finely chopped
2 tablespoons shrimps, cooked
   and chopped
2 tablespoons lemon juice or
   tamarind liquid
1 tablespoon raw sugar
1 cup fish stock or water
1 cup finely chopped fresh tropical
   fruit (papaya, rambutan,
   pineapple, guava, etc.)
salt and pepper

Prepare the fish steaks and lay out in a shallow dish. Blend oil, lemon juice, ginger and seasoning and pour over fish, ensuring that each steak is well coated. Leave for at least 2 hours in the refrigerator.

Grind the peanuts coarsely in a blender or food processor. Heat the oil in a frypan. Add onion, garlic and chilis, and cook until the onion is golden. Add shrimps, ground peanuts, lemon juice or tamarind, raw sugar and stock or water. Stir and gently bring to the boil. Reduce heat and add tropical fruit, adjust seasoning and simmer for 3 minutes. Keep warm.

Barbecue the shark steaks, ensuring that the flesh is not allowed to become too dry by basting with the oil and lemon juice marinade, and until they are evenly cooked on both sides. Serve immediately with the fruit and peanut sauce served separately.
Yield: 6 portions.

CRAB & CRAYFISH

Lobster, crayfish, crab, shrimps and other shellfish, when purchased fresh and live, should be cooked as soon as possible. These are superior in flavor to the frozen or canned variety but, of course, are not always available. They are best cooked by simmering in a rich, flavorful fish stock, or court bouillon, which ensures that flavor is maximised. 2–3 minutes is sufficient for smaller shellfish, 10–15 minutes for larger lobster and crayfish.

To extract the flesh from cooked crabs, allow to cool and then cut through the center of the underside and pull back the soft shell. Scoop the flesh out and then crack the legs and claws carefully to pull out sections of flesh. Some should be retained for garnishing. Flesh may be flaked with a fork or cut into pieces, depending on how it is to be used. The amount of flesh obtained from crabs depends on the species, the season and the sex. In general, female crabs have more flesh than males.

Crab vakasoso

Traditionally cooked in a coconut shell. The recipe is sufficient to fill one large whole coconut.

1 large whole coconut
2 cups cooked crab or shrimps,
   fresh or frozen
1½ cups shredded Chinese
   cabbage (pak choi)
1 medium tomato, finely chopped
1 medium onion, finely chopped
2 tablespoons grated coconut
¼ cup thick coconut cream or
   lighter alternative (page 6)
chives or green onions for garnish

Open the coconut (page 6), remove the flesh, reserving 2 tablespoons of grated coconut flesh. Flake crabmeat coarsely and set aside in a large bowl. Blanch shredded pak choi in salted boiling water for 30 seconds. Drain and cool immediately.

Combine crab, pak choi, tomato, onion and grated coconut. Spoon mixture into the prepared shell and

pour coconut cream over it. Close the shell with coconut lid. Put coconut into a high-sided saucepan containing 2 inches (5 cm) of water, supported upright and preferably not touching the bottom. (An open-ended tuna can makes a suitable support ring.) Cover saucepan and steam the coconut for 10–15 minutes until heated through. Remove coconut lid and top with chopped

Tropical dressed crab

chives or green onions.

If desired, the coconut and the support ring can be transferred to a platter and surrounded with hot cooked rice sprinkled with chopped chives.

Yield: 4 portions.

Tropical dressed crab

1 x 2 lb (800 g) whole crab, fresh or frozen
½ cup diced celery
½ cup peeled and diced cucumber
2 teaspoons lemon juice
salt and pepper
½ cup coconut cream, mayonnaise, or a blend of yogurt, coconut cream and mayonnaise
parsley or dill for garnish

Prepare the crab as directed for Fiji crab (page 40). Put the cooked flesh in a bowl and flake with a fork. Add celery, cucumber, lemon juice, salt and pepper. Fold in coconut cream and spoon the mixture into the crab shell. Arrange attractively, with claws in a folded position, on a large platter. Garnish with chopped parsley or dill sprigs.
Yield: 6–8 portions.

39

reserved shells and set on a flat pan. Bake in a 350°F (180°C) oven until the egg sets — about 10–15 minutes. Serve hot.

Yield: 4 portions.

Note: The crab mixture may be baked in ramekins for individual servings.

Microwave note: Put filled shells on glass plate and cook on medium for 5 minutes. Stand for 2 minutes. Or cook separately for 3 minutes and stand for 2 minutes.

Crayfish with zucchini

8 small zucchini
2 cups salted water
½ cup chopped onion
¼ cup chopped green pepper
4 tablespoons butter or margarine
½ cup flour
1 cup milk, standard or low fat
2 teaspoons lemon juice
1 lb (400 g) cooked crayfish or lobster flesh

Slice zucchini and simmer in lightly salted water for 2 minutes. Drain, cool and reserve liquid. In a saucepan sauté onion and green pepper in butter for 4 minutes. Stir in flour and cook for 1 minute. Slowly stir in milk and reserved cups of liquid. Simmer until thick, stirring occasionally. Stir in lemon juice and crayfish flesh. Fold in zucchini and heat gently.

Serve hot with baked or steamed taro, potato or cooked rice.

Yield: 6 portions.

Microwave note: Lay sliced zucchini in a flat casserole. Add ¼ cup water and cover loosely with plastic wrap. Cook 2 minutes on medium heat and stand for 2 minutes. Drain off liquid into 2-cup measure, adding enough water to equal 2 cups.

Follow standard method of sautéing vegetables and making sauce. Crayfish may be heated for 2 minutes before adding to the sauce. Completed mixture should be heated on medium, stirring at 2 minute intervals.

Crayfish with zucchini

Fiji crab

2 x 1lb (400 g) whole crabs, fresh or frozen
1 medium onion, chopped
1 clove garlic, crushed
2 tablespoons vegetable oil
1 large tomato, finely chopped
2 eggs, well beaten
salt and pepper

Crab is usually bought cooked, but if you are cooking live crabs, plunge whole crab into boiling water and

cook for 15–20 minutes until the shell appears brownish-pink. Plunge into cold water and allow to cool.

Crack claws and legs and remove flesh. Remove flesh from body, taking care to preserve the back shell for final part of the preparation. Rinse shell and dry. Sauté the onion and garlic in oil until golden. Mix all ingredients into the eggs. Divide the mixture into the 2

MEAT DISHES

Eastern-style baked lamb

Although meat bought in most Western countries is of a reasonably good quality, this is not always the case in the tropics. Here toughness and poor flavor may be due to lack of maturing under good storage conditions. Sometimes meat may be contaminated due to exposure in open markets. When bought under these conditions it should be washed in salt water before use.

To make such meat palatable, it requires marinating, spicing, and essentially cooking for a long time. Nowadays, use can be made of these techniques to provide fresh and interesting meat dishes.

Preparation and tenderising

Tenderness and flavor is frequently improved by soaking for a few hours in an acid marinade or a soy sauce mixture. The following marinades could be used for most meats, but it is suggested that an appropriate flavoring be chosen from the spices and herbs recommended for the different meats.

Marinating mixtures

The following are sufficient to marinate 1½ lb (600 g) meat.

Acid
¼ **cup lemon juice**
¼ **cup vegetable oil**
salt and pepper
1 **small clove garlic, crushed**
2 **teaspoons chopped fresh herbs or ½ teaspoon dried mixed herbs**

Mix all ingredients thoroughly. Lemon juice could be replaced with a dry red or white wine.

Soy
2 **tablespoons soy sauce**
¼ **cup vegetable oil**
2 **teaspoons finely chopped onion**
1 **teaspoon finely chopped fresh ginger root or ½ teaspoon ground ginger**

Fruit tenderisers

Cook tough meat at a low temperature 200°F (100°C) with a chopped or sliced tomato, a few slices of Tahitian apple, green apple, chopped green or ripe papaya, kiwifruit or pineapple. However, be careful not to add too much of any of these fruits as they can break down the fibrous texture of the meat if cooked for too long.

LAMB

Always trim excess fat off joints or chops. Cook larger pieces at a lower temperature, 320–350°F (160–180°C). Use marinades to enrich flavor and to tenderize the meat, if necessary.

In addition to the marinades already mentioned, use yogurt with lamb. For 2 lb (800 g) of meat use ½–1 cup of natural unsweetened yogurt flavored with garlic, herbs or spices.

Recommended flavors are: rosemary, turmeric, mint, cardamom, thyme, ginger, sage, lemon, coriander seeds and leaves, soy sauce, oreganum.

Eastern-style baked lamb

5 lb (2 kg) leg of lamb
1 medium onion
1 clove garlic
1 inch (2.5 cm) fresh ginger root, peeled
1 tablespoon soy sauce
1 tablespoon sesame oil
¼ cup vegetable oil
½ teaspoon pepper
pan juices
cornstarch and water

Trim excess fat from meat. Make short slashes using a very sharp knife at even intervals over the surface of the lamb and place in a deep casserole or roasting dish. In a blender, mince the onion, garlic and ginger root. Add soy sauce, both oils and pepper. Blend well and pour over the meat, rubbing the marinade into the slits in the meat. Cover with plastic film and refrigerate for 6–12 hours.

Roast at 350°F (180°C) for approximately 2½ hours, basting several times. Remove roast from pan and set aside to keep hot.

Skim excess fat from pan juices and add some hot water to make sufficient gravy. Estimate the amount of pan juices and add 2 teaspoons cornstarch, mixed to a paste with water to each cup of pan juices. Bring to the boil, stirring constantly.

Carve and serve immediately with hot gravy.
Yield: 8–10 portions.

Microwave note: Place marinated leg of lamb in a covered microwave dish and cook on high for 10 minutes. Reduce heat to medium and cook for a further 20 minutes. Turn leg over and cook for 20 minutes more on medium. Remove and wrap loosely in foil. Allow to stand for 30 minutes before serving.

Banana peanut lamb casserole

A recipe that has its origins in equatorial Africa.

6 green plantains or large unripe bananas
2 lb (800 g) lamb shoulder, cubed
2 tablespoons vegetable oil
1 medium onion, chopped
1 large green pepper, chopped
2 medium tomatoes, chopped
1 cup water
2 tablespoons peanut butter
½ teaspoon chili sauce
salt and pepper

Using a sharp paring knife, peel and slice the plantains. Put in a bowl and cover with cold water and refrigerate for 1–2 hours. Trim any excess fat from lamb and cut into small cubes. Heat oil in large frypan and sauté lamb. Remove to plate and set aside. Sauté onion, green pepper and tomatoes for 3 minutes. Add lamb and cook together for 5 minutes, stirring occasionally. Drain plantain slices and add to pan. Cook for 5 minutes.

Mix water, peanut butter and chili sauce until smooth. Add to the pan

and simmer until almost dry. Season with salt and pepper. Transfer to a casserole and bake at 350°F (180°C) for 10 minutes. Serve hot.
Yield: 6 portions.

Microwave note: Heat a microwave browning dish. Add oil, cover and heat on high for 1 minute. Add lamb and cook on high for 3 minutes, stirring once. Add vegetables, reduce heat to medium and cook for 15 minutes. Add plantain slices and pour over mixture of water, peanut butter and chili sauce. Continue to microwave on medium for 15 minutes.

Cinnamon-scented mango lamb

6 lamb sirloin chops
salt and pepper
3 fresh mangoes
1½ tablespoons melted butter or margarine
flaked cinnamon stick

Wash fresh, ripe mangoes. With a sharp knife, cut a thick slice off each side. (These are often called the 'cheeks' of the mango.) With the tip of the knife, cut the flesh of each cheek into 3–4 slices, being careful not to pierce the skin. Pull the skin away from the flesh, leaving the slices ready for use.

Trim excess fat from chops, if desired. Sprinkle lightly with salt and pepper. Place on a broiler rack. Broil first side until well browned and edges are crisp. Turn chops over and broil for about 3 minutes. Remove from heat and place 3–4 strips of mango on top of each chop. Brush with melted butter and sprinkle with flaked cinnamon stick. Continue broiling until the chops are suitably cooked and the mango lightly browned.
Yield: 6 portions.

Variation: If fresh mangoes are not available, use fresh peaches or nectarines. Canned mango is also suitable.

Opposite: Cinnamon-scented mango lamb

Lamb shanks with tropical barbecue sauce

Coconut lamb casserole

A very special and exciting way to cook lamb.

**2 lb (800 g) lamb shoulder, boned
2 large onions
¼ cup vegetable oil
½ cup white wine
½ cup tomato purée
½ cup water
2 teaspoons fresh marjoram or
    ½ teaspoon dried marjoram
salt and pepper
2 tablespoons cornstarch
¼ cup water
1 cup sour cream or natural
    unsweetened yogurt or low fat
    alternative
1 cup grated fresh coconut or
    ¾ cup desiccated coconut**

Trim excess fat from lamb and cut into cubes. Chop onions into large pieces. Heat oil in a large frypan and sauté onion until golden, then add lamb cubes and stir-fry for a few minutes. Add wine, tomato purée, ½ cup water and seasonings. Simmer, covered, until tender, about 1 hour.

Combine cornstarch and ¼ cup water and stir into lamb. Cook for 5 minutes or until thickened. Just before serving stir in sour cream. Transfer to heatproof serving dish and top with coconut. Place under broiler until the coconut is toasted. Serve immediately with noodles or fettuccine.
Yield: 6 portions.

Variation: Replace coconut with either slivered almonds and pinenuts, or chopped macadamia, pistachio and cashew nuts.

Microwave note: Heat a microwave browning dish according to directions. Add oil. Cover and reheat for 1 minute on high. Add lamb and onion. Cover and cook on high for 3 minutes. Add wine, tomato purée, water and seasonings. Cover and cook on medium for 35 minutes.

Remove from microwave, stir in cornstarch and water. Cook on medium for 2 minutes more. Add coconut and brown under broiler.

Lamb shanks with tropical barbecue sauce

**6 lamb shanks, approx 4 lb (1.8 kg)
½ cup seasoned flour
½ cup vegetable oil**

Sauce:
**½ cup tomato ketchup
½ cup Chinese Hoisin sauce
1 cup water
1 cup onions, sliced
¼ cup honey
½ cup fresh finely chopped
    pineapple
¼ cup cider or white wine vinegar
2 teaspoons dry mustard
1 teaspoon crushed fresh ginger
    root
1 teaspoon ground allspice
1 clove garlic, crushed
salt and pepper**

Trim any excess fat from lamb. Put seasoned flour in a plastic bag and put in shanks one at a time. Shake well to coat evenly. Preheat the oil in a heavy (cast iron) frypan, sear the shanks on all sides and place in a deep casserole dish. Cover and bake in a 375°F (190°C) oven for about 1 hour.

Mix all remaining ingredients together in a pan over gentle heat. Remove meat from oven and, if necessary, drain any excess fat from casserole dish. Pour about half the sauce over the lamb, cover, and return to oven for ½ hour. Baste with remaining sauce every 10 minutes for the next hour. Serve meat and sauce on cooked rice.
Yield: 6 portions.

Minted Hawaiian rack of lamb

6 individual lamb rib roasts
½ cup water
2 tablespoons corn oil
½ cup wholemeal breadcrumbs
¼ cup finely chopped papaya
¼ cup finely chopped macadamia nuts
2 tablespoons freshly grated coconut or 1¼ tablespoons desiccated coconut soaked in 1 tablespoon of water
1 tablespoon honey
1 tablespoon light Hawaiian rum (or similar)
1 tablespoon freshly chopped mint
salt and pepper
extra 1 cup water
pan juices

Put trimmed lamb in a roasting pan with the water. Brush meat with the oil. Bake in 350°F (180°C) oven for 30 minutes. Blend all other ingredients together until they form a paste. Let stand for at least 30 minutes. Remove lamb from oven and carefully coat back of each rib roast with the paste. Place back in roasting pan so that the coated back is exposed. Return to oven and cook for a further 15 minutes. Add 1 cup of water to pan juices and reduce by half. Strain and serve, unthickened, with lamb. Serve hot.
Yield: 6 portions.

Minted Hawaiian rack of lamb

45

Tropical moussaka

Purple eggplant, which is grown extensively throughout the Pacific, has many uses. This dish, a derivative of the traditional Greek moussaka, uses the eggplant skins to encase a richly flavored filling. When cooked, it is turned out onto the serving dish as a mold. This interesting recipe has the advantage of having fewer calories than the traditional moussaka.

2 lb (800 g) medium-sized eggplant
1 tablespoon lemon juice
salt
½ cup vegetable oil
1 large onion, finely chopped
2 cloves garlic, crushed
2 lb (800 g) finely chopped lamb
½ lb (200 g) mushrooms, chopped
extra salt
2 teaspoons fresh rosemary or 1
    teaspoon dried rosemary
1 teaspoon freshly ground black
    pepper
2 teaspoons paprika
1–2 teaspoons salt
1 cup soft wholemeal breadcrumbs
3 eggs, beaten
parsley and slices tomato for
    garnish

Cut eggplant into quarters. With a spoon scoop out the flesh, sprinkle with lemon juice and reserve, leaving about ¼ inch (½ cm) of flesh on the skins. Sprinkle skins with salt and leave to drain for 30 minutes. Put on a baking tray, brush with some of the oil and brown on both sides under the broiler. Leave to cool. Using a fairly deep 4- or 5-cup mold or baking tin, arrange the skins vertically around the sides with the skins against the dish.

Heat remaining oil, sauté onion and garlic, and chopped eggplant flesh, for about 5 minutes. Add meat and stir-fry until brown and crumbly, then add mushrooms, herbs and seasonings. Stir-fry for a few minutes. Drain any fat from the meat and stir in breadcrumbs. Cool before adding eggs. Pack mixture into mold. Smooth top and cover with foil. Place mold in a deep pan of hot water which half covers the sides. Bake at 365°F (190°C) for 45 minutes. Take out of oven and stand for 10 minutes before inverting onto a serving dish. Garnish with parsley and tomato. Serve with fresh tomato sauce (page 90).
Yield: 6 portions.

Note: Avoid, whenever possible, buying pre-chopped lamb as it often has a high fat content. It is preferable to buy cuts such as leg steaks, trim off extra fat, and then chop or mince them yourself.

Lamb, eggplant and okra casserole

A tasty way to use cooked lamb.

1 lb (400 g) cooked lamb, cubed
¼ cup butter or margarine
1 large onion, sliced
2 cloves garlic, chopped
1 cup sliced okra
1 cup peeled and sliced small
    eggplant
¼ cup flour
1½ cups well-seasoned chicken
    stock
1 cup milk, standard or low fat
1 teaspoon fresh finely chopped
    rosemary or dash dried rosemary
1 bay leaf
salt and pepper
½ cup soft breadcrumbs
1 tablespoon melted butter or
    margarine

In a frypan, melt butter and sauté the onion and garlic. Add okra and eggplant and continue cooking until golden, adding extra butter if necessary. Remove vegetables, using a slotted spoon, and put in a bowl. Add flour to remaining juices in the pan, and stir over a medium heat until smooth. Add stock and milk and cook until thickened and smooth, stirring constantly. Add rosemary, bay leaf and seasoning and simmer for 5 minutes.

In a casserole, place alternate layers of lamb and vegetables. Pour sauce over. Lightly fry breadcrumbs in the melted butter or margarine and sprinkle over top of casserole. Bake in 350°F (180°C) oven for 30 minutes or until browned on top.
Yield: 6 portions.

Madras lamb curry

2 lb (800 g) lamb shoulder chops
¼ cup ghee or vegetable oil
1 clove garlic, crushed
1 medium onion, finely chopped
2 tablespoons curry powder, or to
    your taste
½ cup water
1 tablespoon tomato paste
3–4 small tomatoes, peeled and
    chopped
12 fresh curry leaves or 1 bay leaf
sprig of fresh mint
2 teaspoons lemon juice
salt

Trim any excess fat from chops and cut into cubes. Heat ghee in a

saucepan and sauté garlic and onion until golden. Stir in the curry powder and cook for 2 minutes. Add meat cubes and brown slightly. Add water, tomato paste, tomatoes, curry leaves, mint sprig, lemon juice and salt. Stir well and simmer, covered, on a low heat until the meat is tender, about 30–45 minutes. Extra water may need to be added in small quantities to increase the amount of serving liquid in the curry.
Yield: 6 portions.

Microwave note: In a deep casserole sauté the garlic and curry powder in ghee or oil on high for 30 seconds. Then add onion and tomato paste and cook on high for 2 minutes. Add lamb, curry leaves and mint, stir, cover and cook under cover on medium for 15 minutes.

Lamb korma

½ cup unsweetened natural
   yogurt
1 clove garlic, crushed
1 teaspoon crushed fresh ginger
   root
2 lb (800 g) lamb leg chops
6 whole cloves
4 cardamom pods
1½ inch (4 cm) cinnamon stick
4 tablespoons melted ghee or
   vegetable oil
1 large onion, finely chopped
½ cup unsweetened natural
   yogurt
salt
½ cup coconut cream (optional)

Mix together ½ cup yoghurt, garlic and ginger, and brush over lamb chops on both sides. Put in a pan and set aside in refrigerator for several hours.

Crush cloves, cardamom and cinnamon in a pestle or with rolling pin. Heat ghee in large frypan and sauté spices and onion for 4–5 minutes. Add the meat, additional yogurt and salt. Cover and simmer until the meat is tender. If desired, add coconut cream just before serving. Delicious served with cooked rice.
Yield: 6 portions.

GOAT

Goat meat is popular in Mediterranean and many Asian countries. The Indian people introduced goats to Fiji, and agricultural programs in some other Island countries have established goats for meat production. The flavour and texture of goat meat depends on the age of the animal, the best meat coming from goats under 3 years. Goat meat can be substituted in most lamb recipes. It has a darker color, richer flavor and contains less fat than lamb.

Goat curry

1¾ lb (700 g) goat meat
2 tablespoons oil
1 large onion, sliced
2 cloves garlic, crushed
2 teaspoons crushed fresh ginger
   root
4 cardamom seeds
1½ teaspoons ground coriander
1½ teaspoons ground cumin
1½ teaspoons ground fennel seed
½ teaspoon ground black pepper
1 whole chili or to taste
3 tablespoons ground cashew or
   macadamia nuts
3 medium tomatoes, peeled and
   chopped
¾ cup yogurt, natural unsweetened
little water
1 tablespoon lemon juice
½ teaspoon salt

Cut meat into ½-inch (1.5-cm) cubes.

Heat oil in pan, add onions, garlic, ginger and cardamom pods. Stir-fry over medium heat until onions turn golden. Add spices and nuts. Stir-fry for 1 minute. Add tomatoes and simmer until soft. Beat yogurt with a little water and lemon juice, and stir into curry. Add salt, cover pan and simmer over low heat till meat is tender. Serve with rice and mint chutney (page 91).
Yield: 6 portions.

Note: For best flavour, heat whole spices in a pan until crisp and then grind by hand or in coffee grinder.

Braised leg or shoulder of goat

5 lb (2 kg) leg or shoulder goat meat
3–4 cloves crushed garlic
¼ cup oil
6 medium onions, sliced
6 medium carrots, sliced
6 medium tomatoes, peeled
2 bay leaves
1 small piece cinnamon stick
½ cup red wine
3–4 cups vegetable stock
salt and pepper
cornstarch
water
½ cup chopped parsley or
   coriander

Score the surface of the meat with a sharp knife and rub with garlic. Leave for 2–3 hours. Heat the oil in a heavy casserole and brown the meat on all sides. Remove and set aside. Brown the onions and carrots in remaining hot oil. Place meat in casserole. Add tomatoes, spices, wine and stock. Cover with lid. Cook at 300–325°F (160–170°C) for about 2 hours, or until tender. Lift out meat and vegetables and arrange on serving platter. Remove bay leaves and keep hot. Skim fat off stock and measure in cups. Allow 1 tablespoon of cornstarch per cup of liquid. Mix with a little cold water, stir into stock and bring to the boil. Spoon gravy over meat and sprinkle with chopped parsley or green coriander. Serve with a green vegetable and guava jelly (page 88).
Yield: 6 portions.

BEEF

In this section, we have concentrated on dishes which do not require prime cuts of beef, as the use of cuts such as fillet and sirloin would be unusual in many of the Pacific Islands, except in tourist hotels, because of cost.

To develop the flavor of beef, use any of the following herbs and spices: marjoram, ginger, basil, cinnamon, bay leaf, cloves, sage, cumin, oreganum, nutmeg, thyme, mace, curry leaf, mustard seed, coriander leaf, tamarind, garlic, soy.

Beef can be made more tender by marinating for 4–5 hours in one of the following mixtures (sufficient for about 1 lb (400 g) of meat):

Marinades for beef

¼ cup lemon juice or dry red or white wine
¼ cup vegetable oil
½ teaspoon salt
½ teaspoon freshly ground pepper
1 small clove garlic, crushed
OR
2 tablespoons soy sauce
¼ cup vegetable oil
2 teaspoons finely chopped onion
1 teaspoon crushed fresh ginger root
OR
cook tough beef at low temperature — 275°F (140°C) with plenty of tomato or other acidic fruit; chopped green or ripe papaya; pineapple or kiwifruit.

Kebabs

Delicious kebabs can be made out of any tender meat combined with a variety of vegetables or fruit. Fun to make and eat. To make kebabs, cut meat into 1-inch (2.5-cm) cubes. The meat may be marinated in advance in a flavored sauce.

Thread alternating pieces of meat, sliced onion, green or red pepper, eggplant, mushroom and tomato on a skewer. Brush with oil or melted butter. Season well. Broil slowly over a barbecue or hot coals, or

Kebabs

under an electric/gas broiler. As an alternative use cubes of pineapple, papaya, mango or your favorite tropical fruit in place of some of the vegetables.

Kebabs should be served with rice, and preferably a good rich sauce made from wine, tomato, soy sauce and ginger, or ground peanuts.

Beef curry

1 lb (400 g) boneless blade steak
1 medium onion, chopped
2–3 chilis, chopped
¼ cup vegetable oil
1 teaspoon cumin seed
1 teaspoon turmeric
2 tablespoons curry powder
4 cloves garlic, crushed
1 inch (2.5 cm) crushed fresh ginger root
1 teaspoon salt
1 cup water or beef stock
1 medium tomato, chopped
1 large potato, peeled and cubed (see note)

Trim fat from steak and cut into cubes. In a heavy saucepan sauté the onion and chilis in hot oil until the onion is golden. Add cumin, turmeric and curry powder, and stir well. Add steak and brown slightly, then cover and cook for 10 minutes, stirring occasionally. Meanwhile mix garlic and ginger with salt. Add to curry, cover and cook for 5 minutes more. Add water or stock. Stir in tomato and potato, and simmer until potato is cooked. Serve with rice and condiments.
Yield: 4 portions.

Note: Extra chopped vegetables such as long beans, eggplant and carrot may be added. Some of the potato can be substituted with sweet potato, kumara or parsnip, to provide a different taste to this delicious curry.

Microwave note: Put oil in casserole, cover and cook on high for 1 minute. Add onion, chilis, cumin, turmeric and curry, and cook on high for 2 minutes. Add the meat, garlic and ginger and cook on high for 10 minutes. Add water, tomato and potato and stir very well. Cover and cook on medium for 30 minutes.

Opposite: Beef curry

48

Beef and beans

Dried beans and peas, not traditionally eaten in the Pacific Islands, were introduced to Hawaii by the Portuguese and to Fiji by the Indians. Because of their low cost and high food value, nutritionists encourage the use of these foods in local recipes. The following recipe, of Asian origin, is very suitable to regional cuisine.

½ cup dried red beans (soaked for several hours in water, and water discarded) or 1 cup canned, cooked red beans
1 lb (400 g) stewing steak
2 tablespoons lime or lemon juice
1 tablespoon melted butter
1 tablespoon vegetable oil
1 large onion, chopped
1 teaspoon turmeric
½ teaspoon ground cinnamon
1 tablespoon tomato paste or ½ cup tomato purée
1 teaspoon salt

Boil beans until soft. Drain, retaining liquid. Cut meat into ½-inch (1.5-cm) cubes and sprinkle with lemon juice. In a frypan heat butter and oil, and fry chopped onion until golden. Add meat, turmeric and cinnamon, and stir-fry until brown. Put in a large saucepan, add beans, 1½ cups reserved water from the beans, tomato paste and salt. Stir and simmer until meat is tender. Serve with brown rice and pineapple chutney (page 92).
Yield: 4 portions.

Palusami

Palusami is a traditional Samoan dish made from taro leaves, coconut cream and a variety of fillings. Swiss chard or large spinach leaves make a good substitute for taro leaves. The usual filling for palusami is corned beef and onion, but seafood, such as shrimps and fish, are delicious. Palusami may be prepared for individual servings or as a main dish.

24–34 leaves of young taro, Swiss chard or spinach
1 cup coconut cream, or lighter alternative (page 6)
8 oz (200 g) cooked corned beef
1 medium onion, thinly sliced
2 medium tomatoes, thinly sliced salt
extra 1 cup thick coconut cream

Remove central stalk from taro leaves, or slice off half the chard stalk lengthwise. Soften leaves in hot water until pliable. Arrange leaves in order of size so that the smaller leaves are on top. Make sure that any holes in the leaves are covered. For individual servings hold leaves in the palm of the hand to form a cup. For larger servings,

Beef kovu

place leaves in a shallow round bowl.

In both cases, put the first cup of coconut cream and beef in the center of the leaves, add a layer of tomato and onion, season with salt and slowly pour in extra 1 cup of thick coconut cream, lifting the edge of the leaves to prevent this escaping. Fold over the leaves to make a neat parcel. Secure the ends with a toothpick or tie up with cotton or banana fiber. Wrap in foil or in a wilted banana leaf, put in a covered container and bake in a moderate oven for 30–40 minutes or longer for a larger parcel. Alternatively, cook in a steamer. Serve hot or cold.
Yield: 6 portions.

Microwave note: Place prepared palusami in a casserole, cover and cook on medium for 25 minutes. Stand for 5 minutes.

Beef kovu

A recipe from Papua New Guinea.

2 cups sweet potato or plantain
2 medium onions, sliced
3–4 medium tomatoes, sliced
1½ lb (600 g) stewing steak, cubed
2 cups coconut cream, or lighter
   alternative (page 6)
1 teaspoon salt
banana leaves or foil
chopped chives for garnish

Peel and slice sweet potato or plantain into ½-inch (1.5-cm) slices. Slice onions and tomatoes. Combine meat, coconut cream and salt in a bowl. Arrange wilted banana leaves in a broad, shallow dish and carefully pour in the meat mixture. Fold edges together on top and tie securely. Cook in a steamer or in a covered casserole with 1 cup water in a 350°F (180°C) oven for 2–2½ hours.

To serve, place parcel in a serving dish and fold back the leaves carefully. Garnish with chopped chives.

Variation: Use a large sheet of heavy cooking foil in place of banana leaves. Double fold the edges to make a secure seal.

Microwave note: After kovu has

Palusami

been prepared in banana leaves, place in a greased casserole dish, but do not add water. Cook on medium for 40 minutes.

Spiced corned beef

3 lb (1.2 kg) corned brisket of beef
1 teaspoon turmeric
½ teaspoon cayenne pepper
¼ cup brown sugar
½ cup cider or white vinegar
4–5 peppercorns
3–4 whole cloves
1 bay leaf

Rinse the meat and dry thoroughly with paper towel. Combine turmeric and cayenne, and rub well into all surfaces of the meat. Place in a deep, heavy saucepan or Dutch oven.

Combine remaining ingredients and add to meat. Then add enough water to cover meat. Bring to the boil, cover, reduce heat and simmer for 2 hours, or 45 minutes per pound (400 g), until tender. Remove from saucepan to platter. Cover with foil to keep moist and allow to cool at room temperature.
Yield: 6 portions.

Variation: *Orange-glazed.* Prepare and cook meat as directed but shorten the time by 20 minutes. Remove meat from saucepan and place on foil (optional) in a roasting pan. Spread ½ cup orange marmalade thickly over exposed surfaces. Bake at 350°F (180°C) for 20 minutes. Slice and serve.

Eggplant steak

1 large eggplant, peeled
¼ cup milk, standard or low fat
¼ cup seasoned flour
2 tablespoons vegetable oil
4 boneless rib eye steaks
4 teaspoons hot Dijon mustard
basil and green peppercorn
    cheese (recipe below)

Cut peeled eggplant lengthwise into
4½ inch (1.5 cm) slices. Dip in milk,
then in seasoned flour and fry in oil
until crisp and browned. Transfer
to heated serving plates and keep
hot.

Spread steaks with mustard and
broil or pan-fry. Place on top of
eggplant slices. Garnish with basil
and green peppercorn cheese.
Yield: 4 portions.

Basil and green peppercorn cheese

*There are countless variations to the
flavors and colors that can be
achieved with this recipe.*

¾ cup low fat cream cheese
1 teaspoon olive or vegetable oil
2 teaspoons finely chopped fresh
    basil
2 teaspoons finely chopped sun-
    dried tomatoes
1 teaspoon crushed green
    peppercorns
½ teaspoon chili sauce (optional)
salt

Blend all ingredients thoroughly
and chill before use. Can be piped
onto a greased sheet of kitchen
paper in advance of use, or spooned
out immediately before serving.
Excellent as an appetizer on toasted
French bread or similar base.
Yield: 1 cup.

Beef saté with peanut sauce

1½ lb (600 g) beef top round steak
1 cup coconut cream or lighter
    alternative
1 tablespoon sugar
1 tablespoon lemon juice
2 teaspoons soy sauce
2 cloves garlic, crushed
1 small onion, finely chopped
salt

Cut steak into ½-inch (1.5-cm) cubes
and put into a bowl. Combine
remaining ingredients and pour the
marinade over the meat. Refrigerate
to marinate for several hours,
turning the cubes over once or twice.
Drain marinade and thread cubes on
to 6 large skewers or 12 small ones.
Broil over charcoal or in broiler until
well browned. Serve with peanut
sauce (below).
Yield: 6 portions.

Peanut sauce

1 medium onion, finely chopped
2 cloves garlic, crushed
1 teaspoon chopped fresh ginger
    root
2 tablespoons peanut oil
¼ cup peanut butter
2 cups coconut cream, or lighter
    alternative (page 6)
2 tablespoons soy sauce
1 tablespoon lemon juice
1 small chili, de-seeded and
    chopped
2 teaspoons sugar
salt

Sauté the first three ingredients in
peanut oil. Reduce heat and add
peanut butter and coconut cream,
blending well. Stir in remaining
ingredients and simmer for 5
minutes. Do not allow to boil.
Yield: 2½ cups.

Note: Pork fillet or cubed chicken
breast may also be used for saté.

Eggplant steak

PORK

Pork is one of the most important meats of the Pacific Islands with most village communities successfully rearing pigs. Pork may be prepared in numerous ways. The tradition of roasting whole pigs for ceremonial feasts and Fijian lovos is strong, but pork is equally good boiled, barbecued or cut into fine strips and sautéed with vegetables. It can be successfully pickled or smoked. Because of its bland flavor, the choice of flavorings is important.

Recommended flavors are: cardamom, allspice, celery, ginger, sage, clove, coriander, fennel, soy sauce, orange, apple, papaya and pineapple.

Glaze larger cuts of meat with honey, corn syrup or brown sugar.

Glazed corned pork

4–5 lb (1.6–2 kg) corned pork, ham shoulder or leg
1 bunch mixed fresh herbs or 2 teaspoons dried mixed herbs
2 teaspoons whole cloves
½ cup lemon juice
½ cup orange or pineapple juice
½ cup sugar
extra cloves and flaked cinnamon sticks for garnish
fresh pineapple, thinly sliced (optional)

Wrap pork or ham in muslin cloth and tie with string. Place in a deep heavy pot or Dutch oven and cover with water. Add herbs and cloves. Cover and bring to the boil, then simmer for 2½ hours.

When cooked, lift out and remove cloth, and peel away the rind. (This should pull away easily if pork is sufficiently cooked.) Place meat in roasting pan, score surface in criss-cross fashion and stud with extra whole cloves. Mix lemon and orange juice together and pour over meat, then sprinkle the sugar and cinnamon sticks generously over the top.

Bake at 350°F (180°C) for 45 minutes, basting occasionally until the glaze is golden. If required, thin whole slices of fresh pineapple can be laid down the back and baked for a further 15 minutes. Serve hot or cold.
Yield: 8 portions.

Manila pork loin

A traditional Filipino way of cooking pork.

4–5 lb (1.6–2 kg) loin of pork
1 quart (1 liter) boiling water
2 cups sugar, white or brown
1 tablespoon cornstarch
1 cup cider or white vinegar
1¼ cups water
1 teaspoon crushed fresh ginger root
1 small clove garlic, chopped
1 teaspoon salt

Using a sharp knife, score the outer surface of the loin of pork in a closely-spaced criss-cross fashion. Pour the boiling water over the meat, allowing the water to drain away. Place in roasting pan in 500°F (260°C) oven for 30 minutes to allow surface to brown.

Meanwhile make a sweet and sour sauce by combining all remaining ingredients in a saucepan. Place over a medium heat and bring to the boil, stirring constantly. Simmer until thick and clear.

Remove roast from oven and baste with the sauce. Return to oven and roast at 300°F (150°C) for an additional 2½ hours. Serve hot with pan sauce.
Yield: 8 portions.

Pork rourou

6 pork chops, trimmed and boned
1 cup chopped, cooked taro, spinach or chard leaves
6 slices Swiss cheese
¾ cup seasoned flour
1 egg, beaten
1 tablespoon water
2 tablespoons butter
2 tablespoons vegetable oil
¾ cup breadcrumbs
Note: Taro leaves should be cooked for at least 10 minutes.

Prepare the pork chops by trimming excess fat, removing bone and pounding until thin. Place 2 table-spoons of taro on each piece of pork, and top with a thin slice of cheese. Fold in half and secure with a toothpick. Dip pork in seasoned flour, then in the beaten egg to which the water has been added. Coat with breadcrumbs and chill for 1–2 hours. Fry in a moderately hot pan with butter and oil for 5–7 minutes each side. Serve immediately.
Yield: 6 portions.

Pineapple pork in a pastry parcel

This dish makes use of both the most tender and normally the toughest pork meat and uses the tenderising ability of fresh pineapple to produce an exciting contrast of texture and taste. Can be served either hot or cold.

1 lb (400 g) belly of pork, skinned
1 cup chopped fresh pineapple
1 teaspoon ground allspice
½ teaspoon ground coriander
salt
1 cup cider or water
approx ½ lb (200 g) whole pork fillet
salt and freshly ground pepper
1 tablespoon vegetable oil
sheets of pie or filo pastry (enough to make a generous parcel)
1 egg beaten with 2 teaspoons of water
1 teaspoon ground nutmeg

Trim off any excess fat from belly of pork and cut into chunks. Place in a casserole, add pineapple and sprinkle over allspice, coriander and salt. Add cider and stir. Cover and refrigerate for 2 hours. Bake in a 350°F (180°C) oven for about 1 hour, or until very tender. Cool, then place in a food processor and mince roughly.

Remove any sinew from pork fillet, season and place in a frypan with hot oil. Colour lightly on all sides and remove.

Roll out pastry and spread the finely chopped pork and pineapple over half the surface. Place the pork fillet in the middle. Brush the exposed parts of the pastry with the egg and water, and roll the pastry so

Roast honeyed pork

that both sides meet. Seal ends and brush the outside of the pastry with the egg and sprinkle with ground nutmeg.

Place on a greased baking sheet and very lightly score the surface in a diamond pattern, taking care not to cut through the pastry. Bake in a 350°F (180°C) oven for about 40 minutes. Either serve immediately, hot, or leave to cool and refrigerate to serve cold as a buffet item or cold starter to a meal. This dish is delicious with pineapple or mango chutney (page 92).
Yield: 6 portions.

Roast honeyed pork

5 lb (2 kg) shank leg of pork (with bone)
1 tablespoon grated fresh ginger root
2 teaspoons salt
2 teaspoons ground ginger
2 tablespoons vegetable oil
½ cup honey

Score the upper surface of the roast in a criss-cross fashion. Make a pocket by running a sharp knife between the flesh and fat on the top side. Spread the fresh ginger evenly in the pocket.

Mix salt, ground ginger and oil

together and brush all surfaces of the meat. Roast at 350°F (180°C) for 2½ hours, periodically basting with oil mixture and pan juices.

About 15 minutes before it is done, pour the honey over the roast, return to oven and increase the heat to 375°F (190°C) to ensure a golden glaze.
Yield: 6 portions.

GAME MEATS

Game meats are now obtainable in a number of food markets and are also being served by some restaurants. Because of the high cost, you may wish to prepare game meats for that special meal for a few friends. The following recipes for 4 people are ideal for such an occasion.

CROCODILE

Fresh or salt water crocodile are of equally good quality. To prepare, remove the center bone and any obvious pieces of fat. The taste of crocodile can be compared to chicken. It has a mild, appetizing flavor which may be enhanced by marinating in a little oil and lemon juice or white wine. Care must be taken not to overcook.

Spicy Thai crocodile

1¼ lb (500 g) crocodile meat

Sauce:
3 tablespoons teriyaki sauce
3 tablespoons soy sauce
3 tablespoons Mirin wine
1 tablespoon fish sauce
1 tablespoon sesame oil
1 tablespoon chopped fresh
  ginger root
1 cup finely shredded cabbage
1 cup coarsely shredded carrot or
  fine carrot sticks
1 cup snow peas or young sliced
  beans
½ cup thinly sliced red pepper
½ cup toasted cashews or
  macadamia nuts
6 oz (150 g) ribbon noodles or
  other pasta

Cube crocodile meat, removing the center bone and any visible fat. Mix together first 6 ingredients, add to crocodile and marinate for 2–4 hours. Blanch or microwave vegetables for 2–3 minutes. These should be colorful and crisp.

Cook pasta until soft but firm (*al dente*). Place on a platter and arrange vegetables attractively on top, reserving a little red pepper to garnish. Keep hot. Put crocodile and

marinade in a saucepan and cook over a moderate heat for 5 minutes. Stir in nuts and pour over top of pasta and vegetables. Garnish with thin slices of red pepper.
Yield: 4 portions.

Grilled crocodile

1½ lb (600 g) crocodile fillet
pepper
1 clove garlic, juice only
2 tablespoons lemon juice

Remove back bone and butterfly fillets to obtain larger pieces of meat. These should be about ¾ inch (2 cm) thick. Sprinkle with pepper, garlic and lemon juice. Grill, allowing no more than 5 minutes per side. Serve immediately with fresh vegetables or salad. A fruit or tomato chutney (pages 91,92) makes a nice accompaniment.
Yield: 4 portions.

Variation: Pan fry in a little butter or oil.

Colorful crocodile kebabs

Colorful crocodile kebabs

1¼ lb (500 g) crocodile meat
¼ cup lemon juice
2 cloves garlic, crushed
2 tablespoons oil
1 large red pepper
1 large green pepper
12 small fresh mushrooms or
  pineapple pieces
boiled rice
peanut sauce (optional) (page 52)

Cube crocodile into ¾-inch (2–2.5-cm) cubes, depending on the thickness.

Mix lemon juice, garlic and oil. Pour over crocodile and marinate for 2–4 hours. Drain and reserve marinade.

Prepare cubes of red and green pepper, mushrooms or pineapple, roughly the same size as crocodile cubes. Thread pieces of alternate color onto skewers, allowing about 3 per person. Grill about 5 minutes each side, brushing with marinade all the time. Serve on a bed of rice, with or without peanut sauce.
Yield: 4 portions.

KANGAROO

Kangaroo is a very lean meat, having only 2–5% fat as compared with 10–20% in other meats. It has a high protein content and is low in cholesterol.

It can be cooked in many ways. Steaks are grilled and served rare, whilst other cuts make excellent stews and casseroles. Marinating helps to tenderise cuts of wild kangaroo meat and gives flavor to the more tender but less tasty farmed kangaroo.

Kangaroo stew with dumplings

¼ cup olive oil
2 medium onions, finely chopped
2 cloves garlic, crushed
1¼ lb (500 g) kangaroo meat
½ cup cornmeal
black pepper
salt
2 tablespoons chopped sun-dried
  tomatoes
1 tablespoon crushed juniper
  berries or 2 teaspoons ground
  allspice
1½ cups water
1 beef stock cube

Heat oil in a heavy saucepan or casserole. Add onion and garlic, and stir-fry until golden. Cut kangaroo meat into bite-size pieces. Dip in seasoned cornmeal and stir-fry with onions and garlic for 5–7 minutes. Add tomatoes and juniper berries. Add water and stock cube. Cover and bake at 150°C (300°F) for 1½ hours.

Place tablespoonfuls of herb dumplings on top of the stew. Increase temperature to 180°C (350°F) and cook uncovered for 10 minutes; then cover and cook a further 10 minutes. Serve with mashed sweet potatoes, potatoes or yams, and a green vegetable.
Yield: 4 portions.

Variation: Replace water with red wine.

Herb dumplings

1 cup self raising flour
1 tablespoon fresh mixed herbs or
   1 teaspoon dried
½ teaspoon salt
approx ½ cup milk

Sieve flour, mix in herbs and salt. Make a well in the flour and stir in milk until the mixture is of a 'drop' consistency. Using a wet tablespoon, drop mixture in spoonfuls on top of stew. Cook uncovered for 10 minutes, then cover and cook a further 10 minutes.
Yield: 4 portions.

Papaya kangaroo fillets

1½ lb (600 g) kangaroo steaks
1 teaspoon black or colored
   peppercorns
1 teaspoon coriander seeds
1 lemon
1 small papaya or honeydew
   melon
2 teaspoons margarine
½ cup guava jelly (page 88)
¼ cup gin or vodka

Cut kangaroo steaks into serving pieces, allowing about 6 oz (150 g) per person. Grind peppercorns and coriander together and sprinkle on meat. Squeeze lemon juice over meat and leave for 1½ hours. Peel and slice papaya or melon into ¾-inch (2-cm) thick pieces. Grill steaks 5 minutes each side under a hot grill.
   Heat margarine in a pan and fry papaya until slightly brown. Serve steaks on browned fruit slices. Mash guava jelly with a fork and beat in gin. Serve as a sauce with steaks.
Yield: 4 portions.

Variation: Instead of guava jelly use blackcurrant mixed with cassis.

EMU

The emu produces a meat which is high in protein but low in fat and cholesterol. Although the bird is large, its carcass has comparatively little meat on it. For this reason, emu meat tends to be very costly. It responds well to marinating.

Grilled emu with rich brown sauce

1½ lb (600 g) emu saddle fillets
½ cup red wine
2 tablespoons olive oil
1 clove garlic, crushed
potato coins (recipe opposite)
rich brown sauce (recipe opposite)

Trim any sinew or silver skin from the fillets and then cut into ¾-inch (2-cm) slices. Marinate in red wine, olive oil and garlic for 2–4 hours. Prepare potato coins and rich brown sauce. Drain marinade from steaks and grill about 5 minutes each side. Do not overcook. Serve steaks on a bed of potato coins accompanied by rich brown sauce and colorful green and yellow vegetables.
Yield: 4 portions.

Potato coins

4 medium potatoes (unpeeled)
   thinly sliced
oil for deep fat frying

Fry potatoes in hot oil until golden. Drain on absorbent paper.

Rich brown sauce

1 tablespoon oil
1 medium onion, finely chopped
1 lean bacon rasher, finely
   chopped
1 medium carrot, finely chopped
1 stick celery, finely chopped
1 tablespoon tomato paste
2 tablespoons flour
1 cup water
1 beef stock cube
1 bay leaf
red wine

Heat oil in a pan and stir-fry onion and bacon. Add carrot and celery and stir-fry until almost soft. Stir in tomato paste and flour, then slowly add water, stock cube and bay leaf. Cook and stir until thick and smooth. Add red wine just before serving.

Note: Blend or strain the sauce if a creamy consistency is desired.

Grilled emu with mango

1¼ lb (500 g) emu fillet
½ teaspoon ground cloves
½ teaspoon crushed cardamom
   pods
2 teaspoons ground coriander
1 clove garlic, crushed
2 tablespoons low fat yoghurt
rounds of dry toast

Trim any sinew or silver skin from the fillets and then cut in ¾-inch (2-cm) slices. Make a paste of cloves, cardamom, coriander, garlic and yoghurt. Spread on steaks and leave for 1 hour. Grill for about 4 minutes each side. Serve on rounds of dry toast with a selection of vegetables and chutneys. Very quick and easy, and absolutely delicious.
Yield: 4 portions.

Grilled emu with rich brown sauce

CHICKEN

Chicken is used widely in the tropics and lends itself to an almost limitless range of flavorings and stuffings. There are very few herbs or spices that cannot be used. Care is only needed to ensure that the chicken's delicate flavor is not swamped by seasoning. In its simplest form, if roasting, prise free the skin of the breast with the fingers and rub crushed garlic, basil, ginger, lemon or soy sauce on the underneath flesh. Add additional seasoning of this kind on the outside of the skin and put whole cloves of garlic, whole small onions or shallots into the cavity.

In general, basil, tarragon, parsley, garlic, ginger, saffron, coriander, sesame seed, lemon and pineapple add richness to the flavor of chicken in stews, roasts and casseroles.

Marinades for chicken

Marinate chicken pieces or cut up chicken in this basic lemon mixture for 4–5 hours. Sufficient for 2 lb (800 g).

¼ cup lemon juice, fresh pineapple juice, dry white or red wine, or 1 tablespoon soy sauce
½ clove garlic, crushed
¼ cup vegetable or olive oil
salt and freshly ground pepper
½ cup finely chopped ripe papaya (optional)
¼ cup vegetable oil
2 teaspoons finely chopped onion
1 teaspoon crushed fresh ginger root

South seas pineapple chicken

This is a very simple and successful party dish that can be made ahead of time, refrigerated, and then reheated.

4 lb (1.8 kg) chicken thighs and breasts
juice of 1 lemon or lime
¼ cup soy sauce
¼ cup medium dry white wine
2 teaspoons sesame oil
1 clove garlic, crushed
1 teaspoon crushed fresh ginger root
1 teaspoon curry powder
pinch dried thyme
pinch dried oreganum
pinch dried rosemary
freshly ground pepper
¼ cup flour
6 tablespoons butter or margarine
4 medium onions, finely sliced
1 fresh pineapple, peeled and thickly sliced
½ cup toasted slivered almonds for garnish
¼ cup white wine

Remove skin from chicken and place pieces in a flat dish. Combine next 11 ingredients, pour over chicken and marinate for several hours, turning at least twice. Drain chicken and reserve marinade. Dredge chicken in flour and set aside.

In a large frypan, melt 2 tablespoons butter and fry onion slices until golden. Remove to a side dish. Melt a further 2 tablespoons butter and brown the chicken on both sides. Add the reserved marinade, layer onion slices on top, cover and simmer for 30 minutes. Uncover and continue cooking for 15 minutes. In a small frypan sauté the pineapple in the remaining butter and arrange on a heated platter. Place the chicken pieces on top and garnish with almonds. Add the wine to pan juices and simmer briefly. Pour over meat or serve separately.
Yield: 6 portions.

Stuffed chicken legs

An unusual and easily prepared dish which is ideal for a party.

12 chicken legs or drumsticks
¼ cup vegetable oil
3 tablespoons lemon juice
1 clove garlic, crushed
salt
freshly ground pepper
1 cup cooked taro or spinach
¼ teaspoon ground nutmeg
2 teaspoons butter or coconut cream
1 tablespoon vegetable oil
Note: Taro leaves should be boiled for at least 10 minutes.

Insert the tip of a very sharp knife at the top (bulbous end) of each leg or drumstick to separate the flesh from the bone, forming a pocket.

Combine next 5 ingredients to make a marinade and pour over legs. Allow to marinate for 4 hours, turning legs occasionally. Mash or blend taro or spinach, add nutmeg and butter, and blend until smooth. Adjust salt if necessary.

Drain chicken, reserving marinade. Put a spoonful of taro purée into the pocket of each leg and arrange in a flat baking dish. Brush with oil and marinade. Bake at 375°F (190°C) for 20 minutes or until tender.
Yield: 6 portions.

Microwave note: Prepare as directed. Preheat browning dish and cook on high for 2 minutes. Turn legs over, cover loosely with paper towel and finish cooking on high, allowing 6 minutes per pound (400 g). Stand 7 minutes. Test for tenderness. (If desired, sprinkle with microwave browning powder before cooking.)

Opposite: South seas pineapple chicken

Golden chicken

Golden chicken

5 lb (2 kg) chicken pieces
1 teaspoon pepper
1 tablespoon ground ginger
¼ cup vegetable oil
3 cardamom pods (seeds only)
2 tablespoons cornstarch
2 cups yogurt, natural or low fat
½ cup light cream or 2 table-
**   spoons vegetable oil**
2 teaspoons turmeric
1 teaspoon salt
2 medium onions, finely chopped

Remove skin from chicken pieces.
Rub pepper and ginger into each
piece. Brush with a little oil and
lightly brown in a hot oven or under
the broiler.

Arrange chicken pieces in a
shallow baking dish. Pound cardamom pods and remove seeds. Mix
cornstarch to a paste with a little
yogurt and add to remainder. Put in
a saucepan, heat and stir until
thickened. Add cream or oil, turmeric, salt, cardamom seeds and
onion. Mix very well and then pour
over chicken.

Cover with foil and bake at 325°F
(160°C) for 1 hour. Remove foil for
the last 15 minutes. Serve with
steamed rice and tomato chutney
(page 91).
Yield: 6 portions.

Chicken curry

4 lb (1.6 kg) broiler chicken
3 tablespoons vegetable oil
1 teaspoon fennel seeds
5 cardamom pods
1 inch (2.5 cm) cinnamon stick
1 medium onion, chopped
6 curry leaves (optional)
½ teaspoon crushed fresh ginger
**   root**
3 cloves garlic, crushed
3 whole cloves
1 teaspoon turmeric
1 teaspoon chili powder or fresh
**   chilis**
2 teaspoons curry powder
1 teaspoon salt
2 cups chicken stock or water
2 sprigs coriander (optional)

Cut all flesh from carcass. Discard
any fat. Put bones, loose skin and

wing tips in deep pot, covering with
water, and boil to make stock.
Meanwhile cut flesh into 2-inch
(5-cm) pieces.

In a large saucepan, heat oil and
fry fennel, cardamom and cinnamon
for 1 minute. Add onion and curry
leaves and fry until onion is golden.
Add ginger, garlic and cloves, and
cook for 3 minutes. Stir in chicken,
turmeric, chili, curry powder and
salt. Cook for about 10 minutes,
stirring occasionally. Add enough
chicken stock or water to half cover
mixture. Cover with lid and cook
until tender, stirring occasionally.
Add coriander for extra flavor. Serve
hot with rice and condiments. Whole
spices may be removed before
serving, if desired.
Yield: 6 portions.

Microwave note: Proceed as
directed for preparing chicken and
stock. Put oil in a glass casserole
and cook the spices and onion on
high, adding them 2 or 3 at a time.
Cook for about 4 minutes. Then add
chicken and cook on high 8 minutes.

60

Cover with stock and cook 25 minutes on medium. Stand for 10 minutes. Test for tenderness and, if necessary, cook on medium for another 5 minutes. Best when cooked in advance and re-heated to desired temperature at serving time.

Roast capon with eggplant stuffing

5 lb (2 kg) capon or roasting chicken
2 lean bacon rashers, chopped
1 small onion, chopped
½ clove garlic, finely chopped
1½ cups eggplant, peeled and diced
¼ cup currants or raisins
½ cup cooked rice
2 tablespoons tomato purée
¼ teaspoon ground coriander
½ teaspoon grated lemon rind
salt and pepper

Put the chopped bacon in an un-heated frypan, then place on medium heat. As bacon begins to cook, add

Roast capon with eggplant stuffing

onion and sauté until golden. Add garlic, eggplant and currants. Stir-fry until eggplant is cooked but not too soft and mushy. Add remaining ingredients and stir well.

Spoon mixture into chicken cavity and truss capon. Place in roasting pan and bake at 450°F (230°C) for 15 minutes, then reduce to 350°F (180°C) and continue roasting for 2½ hours or until tender. Stand 15 minutes, well covered, before carving.
Yield: 6 portions.

Note: Stuffing is also suitable for roasting chicken or small turkeys.

Chicken roasted Szechuan-style

Serve with fresh pineapple pieces and hot rice salad.

5 lb (2 kg) roasting chicken or capon
1 clove garlic, crushed
2 teaspoons crushed ginger root
1 tablespoon soy sauce
¼ cup vegetable oil
1 tablespoon sesame oil
1 chili, de-seeded and finely chopped

Rinse and pat chicken dry. In a blender combine remainder of the ingredients. Brush cavity, outside and between breast skin and flesh, with the marinade and leave for 4 hours. Place chicken in a baking pan and roast at 350°F (180°C) for 2 hours, basting several times to ensure an even golden color.
Yield: 6 portions.

Microwave note: Place marinated bird in a glass roasting dish and cook on high 7 minutes per pound (400 g), turning and basting 3 times. Stand 10 minutes, covered.

Chicken lolo suvu

This delicious spicy recipe, from Burma originally, depends on dhal (split peas) and coconut cream for its unique flavor. Preparation needs to begin the day before serving. It provides an excellent addition to a buffet, luau or island feast.

Preparation of dhal (a day ahead)

8 oz (200 g) split yellow peas or arahar dhal
2–3 cups water
dash salt

Wash the dhal, put in a container and cover with water. Soak for 4–5 hours. Drain off the water and measure. If necessary, add extra water to make up to 2–3 cups to cover dhal and cook for 40 minutes until soft and mushy. Skim off any white froth that forms during cooking. Reduce dhal to a purée by rubbing through a sieve, or by blending. Season with salt. Cover and refrigerate until needed.

Preparation of chicken (day ahead)

5 lb (2 kg) chicken cut into serving pieces
2½ cups water
½ cup butter or margarine
1½ cups finely chopped onion
2½ tablespoons garam masala (page 9) or other strongly spiced curry powder
2 teaspoons turmeric
1 tablespoon crushed green ginger root
10 cloves garlic, crushed
approx 1 rounded tablespoon salt
1 cup chicken stock
2 chicken bouillon cubes
1 cup peeled and mashed tomatoes

Cut the flesh off the chicken breasts, thighs and backs. Put all bones and wings into a pot, cover with water, and boil until stock is reduced to about 1 cup. Set aside.

Heat butter in a large frypan. Add onions and sauté until golden brown. Add garam masala, turmeric, ginger, garlic and salt, and stir-fry 1–2 minutes over medium heat. Add chicken and stir-fry until browned. Add chicken stock, bouillon cubes and tomatoes, and simmer until chicken is just tender. Cool and refrigerate overnight. (This helps the flavor develop.)

Day of dinner

4 large onions, sliced in rings
milk
flour
vegetable oil
2 cups rice
1 cup thick coconut cream, or lighter alternative (page 6)

Cut onions into thin rings, dip in milk and then flour. Fry in hot oil until golden brown and crisp. Drain on absorbent paper and keep hot. Cook rice.

Thirty minutes before serving time, heat the chicken to simmering point and stir in the dhal. Five minutes before serving, add the coconut cream. Heat to boiling point. Serve in a large deep platter accompanied by rice and crisp onion rings.
Yield: 6 portions.

Crispy chicken with guava sauce

6 chicken breasts, boned
4 tablespoons light soy sauce
1 tablespoon sesame oil
½ cup dry white wine
1 cup chicken stock
2 tablespoons lemon juice
2 tablespoons sugar
1 tablespoon cornstarch
salt
8 oz (200 g) prepared guava slices
6 green onions, chopped

Batter:
2 oz (50 g) flour
2 oz (50 g) cornstarch
½ teaspoon salt
1 egg, beaten
½ cup water
oil for frying

Cut each chicken breast into 3–4 pieces. Mix soy sauce, sesame oil and wine, and add chicken pieces. Leave to marinate for 2 hours. Put stock, lemon juice and sugar in a saucepan and bring to the boil. Add guava slices and cook until just tender. Drain marinade off chicken pieces. Mix a little marinade with the cornstarch. Season with salt and add to guavas with the green onions. Stir well and bring to the boil.
Batter: Sift flour, cornstarch and salt. Add beaten egg and water to make a fairly thick batter. Rest for an hour. Heat oil in saucepan or deep frypan. Dip chicken into batter and fry until lightly brown and crisp. Drain on absorbent paper and keep hot. Serve chicken pieces with hot guava sauce and rice.

Variation: Replace chicken with pork fillet and guava with pineapple.

VEGETABLES

Many tropical vegetables have an excellent flavor and texture, but as with all vegetables, proper preparation and cooking is necessary. Some dark, leafy spinach-like vegetables can be used raw in salads, quickly cooked in a little boiling water, or 'sweated' in a little butter or oil.

In general, green vegetables should be boiled for a maximum of 5 minutes. Some of the tropical leafy vegetables like taro leaves, bele (edible hibiscus leaf), and ota (edible ferns) are best cooked in plenty of lightly salted boiling water, with the lid off the pot. (This allows acids in the vegetables to disperse and

preserves the color). Taro leaves should be boiled for at least 10 minutes. This breaks down the oxylate content in the leaves and other substances which may sting and irritate the mouth and throat.

All green vegetables have a high mineral and vitamin content. Red and yellow fruits, and vegetables such as pumpkin and peppers, are also excellent sources of vitamins A and C. Most tropical beans and gourd-like vegetables, such as Chinese marrow, have similar food values to their temperate climate equivalents.

Starchy root vegetables, like manioc and taro, make a pleasant change from potatoes in most recipes, and are excellent in potato and other salads. Manioc makes particularly good chips which retain their crispness.

For more detailed information on the food values of tropical vegetables see page 98.

Taro, pineapple and bacon chips

Taro cakes with roast pork

Manioc (cassava) or taro cakes

3 cups mashed or grated cooked manioc, taro or potato
2 teaspoons grated onion
2 teaspoons chopped parsley
1 egg, beaten
salt and pepper
flour
vegetable oil

Mix manioc or taro with onion, parsley, egg, salt and pepper. Form into cakes and roll in flour. Fry in hot oil on both sides until golden brown. Serve hot as a starter with a spicy sauce or tropical salsa, or in place of potatoes with main courses. **Yield**: 6 portions.

Variation: Replace 1 cup of manioc or taro with 1 cup of flaked cooked fresh or smoked fish, minced meat or chicken. Serve meat or fish cakes with a fresh tomato sauce (page 90).

Sweet potato soufflé

3 tablespoons butter, melted
1 tablespoon milk
2 tablespoons grated onion
½ teaspoon ground cinnamon
salt and pepper
3 cups mashed sweet potato
3 eggs

Add 2 tablespoons melted butter,

milk, onion, cinnamon, salt and pepper to mashed sweet potato. Mix well. Separate the eggs and beat the whites until stiff, then beat the yolks until frothy. Fold first the egg yolks into the potato mixture, and then the egg whites.

Put into a deep greased round baking dish, ideally a soufflé dish, brush the top with the remaining melted butter and bake in the oven in a pan of water at 325°F (160°C) for about 30–40 minutes, or until the soufflé is well risen and golden brown. Excellent with pork or cold meats.
Yield: 6 portions.

Taro, pineapple and bacon chips

This delectable combination can be used as a vegetable but is equally useful as a snack dish whilst sipping your favorite cocktail.

1 lb (400 g) taro, peeled
4 fresh pineapple slices
4 bacon rashers
1 tablespoon vegetable oil
1 tablespoon butter or margarine
4 green onions, chopped
freshly ground pepper
sliced lemon and dill sprig for garnish

Cut taro into ½-inch (1.5-cm) slices and steam or boil until tender but firm. Drain, spread to cool, then cut into chips, 1 inch x ½ inch (2.5 cm x 1.5 cm).

Cut pineapple slices into similar sized pieces. Cut bacon into ½-inch (1.5-cm) wide strips. Heat oil and butter in a heavy frypan and fry taro chips until golden. Remove, drain on paper towel and keep hot in 200°F (100°C) oven. In the same pan, sauté pineapple pieces until golden, transfer to oven pan and keep hot. Fry bacon until crisp. Drain well on paper towel.

In a bowl, quickly combine the hot chips, pineapple and bacon and toss lightly with green onions. Sprinkle with pepper. Transfer to serving bowl, garnish with lemon slices and dill sprig, and serve immediately. **Yield**: 6 portions.

Microwave note: Prepare and cook as directed. Set aside until needed. Put into serving dish and, just prior to serving, cook 2 minutes on high to bring to serving temperature.

Spiced island vegetables

In this delicious vegetarian dish, coconut and spices enhance the flavor of vegetables.

½ cup split peas
3 cups water
salt
2 tablespoons vegetable oil
1 small onion, sliced
5 cups fairly firm vegetables, cut in strips (Chinese cabbage stalks, carrots, white radish (daikon), French or long beans (try to have four kinds but keep each one separate)
3–4 curry leaves (optional)
2 cups water
½ cup grated coconut or 3 table-spoons desiccated coconut
½ cup coconut cream
½ teaspoon salt
½ teaspoon grated fresh ginger root
½ teaspoon cumin seed
½ teaspoon coriander seed
1–2 small chilis or ¼–½ teaspoon chili powder
1 clove garlic, peeled

Soak split peas for half an hour and cook in salted water until soft, then drain. Heat oil in frypan or wok, sauté sliced onion for a few minutes, and then add the vegetables one at a time, starting with the firmer kinds. Stir-fry each for a minute before adding the next. Add curry leaves and water, and simmer until vegetables are just soft but still firm. Stir in split peas.

In a blender or food processor put coconut, coconut cream, salt and remainder of ingredients. Blend until smooth. Stir into the vegetables and simmer for a minute or two. Do not overcook. Serve with rice and a fresh tomato chutney (page 91).
Yield: 6 portions.

Spicy Chinese beans

The idea for this dish comes from the Shanghai region of China. It is equally good served hot or cold.

**10 oz (250 g) young French or long
  beans**
2 teaspoons salt
1½ teaspoons black peppercorns
2 tablespoons sesame oil
**1–2 medium-sized fresh or dried
  chilis**
3 tablespoons wine vinegar
2 tablespoons sugar
**1 inch (2.5 cm) fresh ginger root,
  crushed**
1 clove garlic, crushed

Trim tops and ends of beans and cut in half or quarters, depending on size. Blanch in boiling water for about 2 minutes. Drain and rinse in cold water. Put in a bowl of cold or iced water, add salt and leave for 15 minutes. Drain off water and put beans in serving dish.

Heat a heavy frypan or wok, put in peppercorns and stir with a wooden spoon until you smell their fragrance. Add sesame oil, half the chili, vinegar and sugar. Simmer together for half a minute. Remove pan from heat and stir in ginger, garlic and remaining chili. Pour over beans, toss and chill if using for a salad, or heat to serve as a vegetable.
Yield: 6 portions.

Note: For those who do not like spicy hot food, use just one quarter of the chilis or leave out altogether.

Spinach stuffed tomatoes

An attractive vegetable dish which can be served alone or with main courses.

6 large tomatoes
**1½ cups cooked mashed spinach
  or taro leaves (rourou)**
**2 tablespoons thick coconut cream,
  or lighter alternative (page 6)**
dash ground nutmeg
salt

**Note: Taro leaves must be boiled
for at least 10 minutes**

Cut tops off the tomatoes or make a serrated edge with the point of a knife. Scoop out the pulp and keep for other tomato-based dishes. Add coconut cream, nutmeg and salt to spinach. Put the mixture in the tomato cups and place in a shallow baking dish. Cover with foil and bake at 350°F (180°C) for about 10 minutes. Do not overcook as tomatoes will lose their shape.
Yield: 6 portions.

Spiced island vegetables

Karela mixed vegetables

This recipe uses the karela or bitter melon which adds sharpness to the flavor of other vegetables. It is a favorite food of all Asian people living in the Pacific.

6 oz (150 g) karela
8 oz (200 g) celery
1 lb (400 g) Chinese cabbage (pak choi) or sensopai
2 tablespoons vegetable oil
2 cloves garlic, crushed
1½ teaspoons crushed fresh ginger root
½ cup water
1 teaspoon salt

Scrape the skin off the karela fruits, cut in half, remove the seeds and slice crosswise. Cut celery and Chinese cabbage stalks into ½-inch (1.5-cm) pieces. Shred the leaves. Heat the oil and stir-fry the garlic and ginger for a few minutes over medium heat. Add the karela and cabbage stalks and stir-fry for about 5 minutes. Finally add the cabbage leaves, water and salt. Mix well. Cover the pan and steam until all vegetables are crisp but tender — about 4 minutes.
Yield: 6 portions.

Cucumber with basil and tomato

An excellent dish to serve with chicken or fish.

1¾ lb (700 g) cucumbers
2 teaspoons salt
4–5 green onions
3 tablespoons vegetable oil
¼ cup cream (optional)
½ cup natural unsweetened yogurt
salt and freshly ground black pepper
1 tablespoon chopped basil leaves
1 lb (400 g) tomatoes

Peel cucumbers and scoop out large seeds. If very young, leave seeds. Cut into ½-inch (1.5-cm) pieces. Sprinkle with salt and leave to drain for 20 minutes, then rinse under cold water and dry. Cut green onions into 1-inch (2.5-cm) pieces. Heat oil and stir-fry cucumber over high heat. Mix cream with yogurt and stir into cucumber. Season with salt and pepper and half the basil. Peel, de-seed and dice tomatoes. Fold into the cucumber mixture and simmer over low heat for 5 minutes. Serve garnished with remaining basil.
Yield: 6 portions.

Stuffed eggplant

Small- to medium-sized eggplants grow in profusion in tropical countries. This dish is excellent prepared in advance for a luau or buffet.

3 medium-sized eggplants
1 medium onion, chopped
1 clove garlic, crushed
½ teaspoon ground or cracked coriander seed
¼ cup vegetable oil
½ lb (200 g) ground lamb
1 tablespoon chopped parsley
salt and pepper
½ cup soft breadcrumbs
2 tablespoons tomato purée
1 egg, beaten

Trim ends off eggplant and cut in half lengthwise. Scoop out flesh leaving about ¼ inch (0.5 cm) inside. Chop flesh and set aside. Arrange eggplant shells in a close-fitting casserole dish. (This helps keep shape and contents in place.)

In a large frypan, sauté onion, garlic and coriander in oil. Add eggplant flesh and ground lamb. Sauté for about 5 minutes, then add parsley, salt and pepper, breadcrumbs and tomato purée. Stir well and cook for 3 minutes more. Remove from heat and stir in egg. Spoon filling into shells. Cover with foil or lid and bake at 350°F (180°C) for 45 minutes. Remove cover and brush surface with oil. Return to oven to brown. Serve hot.
Yield: 6 portions.

Microwave note: Prepare ingredients as directed. Sauté all vegetables, spices, meat and tomato purée in preheated browning dish for 5 minutes. Stir in breadcrumbs and egg. Spoon into shells. Cover loosely with plastic wrap. Cook on high 10 minutes, turning twice. Remove wrap and stand 5 minutes, then brush with oil and place in broiler to brown top. Serve.

Variation: Substitute ground beef for lamb, and cooked rice for breadcrumbs.

Rourou (taro leaves) Meredane

Taro is the favorite root crop in Polynesia. Roots and leaves are always served at feasts. Ways of preparing and cooking the young leaves and stems is the cook's secret in all countries! The basic ingredients used in taro leaf dishes are coconut cream, salt and onion. The Chinese immigrants to Hawaii probably introduced the spicing of taro leaves — luau — with garlic and ginger. The idea then found its way to Fiji. In this recipe, Meredane combines the cookery crafts of three Pacific countries.

1½ lb (600 g) young taro leaves
coconut cream made from 2 grated coconuts and 2 cups water
1 medium onion, finely chopped
½ teaspoon crushed garlic
1 teaspoon crushed fresh ginger root
salt

Pull the stalks off the leaves, cut in half and wash well. Pour coconut cream into a large saucepan. Add onion, garlic, ginger and salt, and bring to the boil. Put taro leaves into saucepan and boil very fast with lid off for 15–20 minutes.
Yield: 6 portions.

Note: Taro leaves should always be boiled for at least 10 minutes in water or coconut milk as they contain an acrid substance which can sting the mouth. This is more prevalent in old leaves. Good quality taro leaves should feel soft and pliable. Taro leaves are high in vitamins and the acridity is harmless to health.

Opposite: Stuffed eggplant

Indonesian pumpkin

Pumpkin grows throughout the Pacific. It thrives equally well in the hot summers of the temperate climates and throughout the year in the tropics. Many of the Pacific Island and oriental pumpkin recipes include coconut.

1½ lb (600 g) peeled and de-seeded pumpkin
2 tablespoons vegetable oil
1 large onion, chopped
1½ tablespoons chopped fresh ginger root
2 cloves garlic, chopped
1 tablespoon chopped coriander leaves
½ teaspoon salt
1½ tablespoons soy sauce
1½ cups medium coconut cream, or lighter alternative

Cut the pumpkin into ½-inch (1.5-cm) cubes. Heat oil, add onion, ginger, garlic and coriander. Stir-fry for 1 minute. Add pumpkin and continue to stir-fry for 5 minutes. Mix salt and soy sauce with coconut cream. Pour over pumpkin and simmer on low heat until soft.
Yield: 6 portions.

Note: The addition of chilis turns this dish into a hot vegetarian curry.

Curried taro, yam, breadfruit, potato

This is a new and interesting way of preparing staple, starchy vegetables. Serve as an accompaniment with cold meats or as an extra dish for a curry menu.

2 lb (800 g) taro, yam, breadfruit or potato, or a combination of the four
1 tablespoon butter
2 tablespoons vegetable oil
1 inch (2.5 cm) fresh ginger root, crushed
3 cloves garlic, crushed
1 teaspoon ground cumin
4 cardamom pods
½ teaspoon ground cinnamon
¼ teaspoon chili powder
2 teaspoons ground coriander

Peel chosen vegetable or vegetables.

Cut into pieces and steam or boil until half cooked. Cool and cut into ½-inch (1.5-cm) cubes. Heat butter and oil in a large pot or frypan. Add ginger and garlic and stir-fry over a low heat for 2–3 minutes. Add the prepared vegetables and spices, and toss spices until well mixed. Put a lid on the pan and steam for a few minutes.
Yield: 6 portions.

Baked savory breadfruit

In 1792 Captain Bligh carried breadfruit plants by sailing ship from Tahiti to the Caribbean islands. Two centuries later, this wonderful recipe was found in Jamaica and adapted to suit Pacific Island tastes.

1 large breadfruit
2 green onions, chopped
1 medium onion, chopped
1 green pepper, chopped
1 red pepper, chopped
2 tablespoons vegetable oil
2 tablespoons chopped parsley
1 tablespoon chopped fresh mixed herbs or 1 teaspoon dried mixed herbs
1 cup cooked meat (pork, ham or corned beef), cubed
1 beef bouillon cube
1 cup hot water
1 cup cooked and diced carrots
salt and pepper
1 egg, beaten

Wash breadfruit and puncture deeply in about 6 places. Bake at 350°F (180°C) for approximately 1½ hours or until soft. A carving fork

should pierce it easily.

In a large frypan, sauté the onions and peppers in oil for 5 minutes in a large frypan. Add chopped herbs and cook a few more minutes. Cut meat into ½-inch (1.5-cm) cubes and stir into pan. Dissolve bouillon cube in water and add to pan with carrots. Add salt and pepper, stir well and simmer for 15 minutes.

Cut the top off the baked breadfruit and scoop out the pulp, leaving a shell of about ½-inch (1.5-cm) thickness inside. Grate the pulp in a food processor or by hand and fold into the hot onion and pepper mixture. Stir in the beaten egg. Spoon all into the breadfruit shell. Replace the top and secure with toothpicks and wrap in heavy foil. Bake at 425°F (220°C) for 30–40 minutes. Unwrap, cut into wedges and serve hot.
Yield: 6 portions.

Edible seaweed

Seaweeds of many kinds are eaten by most Pacific Island peoples. The Hawaiians include 12 different kinds of seaweeds, or limu, in their daily meals. Other countries use these nutritious vegetables to a lesser extent. In Fiji, four different kinds are regularly sold in the markets.

All seaweeds have a high food value as they contain vitamins and the important mineral, iodine. Most varieties are eaten raw, usually chopped up and flavored with onion, chili, and lime or lemon juice, although specific flavors are used in preparing different varieties. The Fijians flavor a small grape-like seaweed, nama, with fermented coconut (kora). Another hair-like kind, lumi, is boiled in coconut cream to make a jelly.

In general, seaweeds are eaten as a relish with fish and shellfish. They add a unique flavor and texture to all seafoods and it is worthwhile seeking traditional advice from Pacific Islanders on the preparation and use of these unusual vegetables.

FRUITS & DESSERTS

Soursop with bananas and pineapple

Tropical fruits, prepared and served in different ways, provide the perfect ending to a meal.

Numerous interesting dessert salads, low in calories and high in taste, can be made by simply combining fruits of varying flavors.

The choice of the dessert is important and should ensure that flavor and texture contrast with earlier dishes. For example, Flaming fruit (page 72) would be delicious after a heavier main course which included Manila pork (page 54), whereas a menu which centered on

seafood could end with crisp and tangy banana orange pie (page 76).

The recipes in this section have been chosen for their fine flavor and easy preparation. A number have their origin in the traditional cooking of the Pacific Islands. Many can be prepared in advance and stored in the refrigerator.

Tropical fruit combinations

Vary the taste of fruits by serving with a sauce made from another fruit of complementary flavor. The

following suggestions will enable you to put together the right kinds of fruits needed to make delicious fruit salads.

Soursop with banana or pineapple

Peel a ripe soursop. Discard the black seeds, mash up the pulp or blend, and then rub through a sieve or strainer. Mix the purée with fruit in the proportions of 1 cup of purée to 3 cups of prepared fruit. Test the flavor and add sugar or lemon juice, if needed.

Note: Extra purée may be frozen in ice cube trays or other containers and kept for future use.

Guava and bananas

Cut ripe guavas into slices. Put in a saucepan or microwave dish. Add 4 tablespoons of water to 1 cup of fruit and cook until soft — about 5 minutes in a microwave on high. Mash or blend and then rub through a sieve or strainer. To every cup of purée add 1 tablespoon each of sugar and lemon juice. Mix the purée with banana slices and serve chilled.

Note: Some guavas are sweeter than others and may not require sugar. Lemon juice develops the flavor. Extra purée may be frozen.

Avocado with lime and honey

Peel 2 medium-sized avocados, about 8 oz (200 g) each, and sieve or blend the soft flesh. Add 1 tablespoon honey, 4–5 tablespoons of lemon juice and a pinch of salt. Mix or blend until well combined. Serve as a sauce with ice cream; mix with an equal quantity of whipped cream or yogurt and use as a sauce with fruits; or mix with an equal quantity of soursop purée to provide the base for an exotic ice cream or cold dessert recipe.

Note: Use within one day as avocado changes flavor and color.

Orange with papaya, mango or cantaloupe melon

Peel, remove pith and segment 2 oranges. Combine with 3–4 cups ripe papaya or mango, cut into cubes. Pour over a sauce made from the juice of 1 orange and half a lemon or lime.

Variation: Add ½ cup of chopped crystallised ginger.

Watermelon, pineapple and mint

Cut melon into balls or cubes to make 2 cups. Add 2 cups cubed fresh pineapple and ¾ cup lemon mint syrup. Just before serving, add ¼ cup fresh mint leaves.

Melon ball salad

Marinate equal quantities of watermelon balls and cantaloupe melon in lemon syrup. Serve in a half cantaloupe shell garnished with a sprig of mint.

Flavoring fruit salads and desserts

Most fruit salads need some sweetening. This may be added as a syrup, melted honey or caster sugar. A home-made syrup, which can be stored in the refrigerator, is the best sweetener.

Avocado with melon balls

The crisp texture and red color of watermelon complements avocado. Soak melon cubes or balls in the following marinade for one hour or more, drain well and serve in the cavity of ripe avocados.

Marinade:
Boil ¼ cup mint leaves in about ¾ cup boiling water for 2–3 minutes. Cool. Strain and mix mint water with ¼ cup lemon juice.

Basic syrup

1 cup sugar or an equivalent amount of artificial sweetener
1½ cups water
thin rind (zest) ¼ lemon and orange

Heat sugar and water to boiling point. Add lemon and orange peel. Simmer for a few minutes. Leave peel in syrup. Cool and store in bottle. Must be refrigerated. If using artificial sweetener, add peel to water and simmer as above. Cool, add sweetener and store as above.

Orange ginger syrup
To basic syrup add ¼ cup fresh orange juice or 1 tablespoon concentrate, and 1 tablespoon finely chopped crystallised ginger.

Lemon syrup
Add ¼ cup lemon or lime juice to basic syrup.

Lemon mint syrup
Add ½ cup chopped fresh mint to basic syrup and simmer for 5 minutes. Strain and add 2 tablespoons lemon juice.

Other ways of flavoring fresh fruit

A little alcohol, either in the form of spirits or a liqueur, is often used to develop the natural flavors of fruit. It is important to choose a spirit with a flavor which complements the fruit. Be careful not to use too much as it can swamp the natural flavor. Use about 1 tablespoon of alcohol to a 4-cup-sized bowl of fruit.

Suggested combinations:
Papaya and cantaloupe — brandy, rum (light or dark), port
Guava — any orange based liqueur, port
Pineapple — most fruit or herb flavored liqueurs
Soursop, passion fruit — orange-based liqueurs and Kirsch
Mango — brandy, Kirsch, Drambuie
Citrus — sherry, rum, Scotch whisky
Mixed fruit salad — Scotch whisky or bourbon

Avocado with melon balls

70

Minted pineapple

6 cups fresh pineapple, cubed
3 tablespoons lime or lemon juice
½ cup crème de menthe or a
   strong peppermint essence
   mixed with ½ cup basic syrup
   (page 70)
green food coloring, if desired
mint leaves for garnish
lightly sweetened and colored
   whipped cream, if desired

Put prepared fruit in a bowl. Mix
with lemon juice and crème de
menthe until all pieces are covered.
Refrigerate for at least 1 hour before
serving, stirring once or twice. Serve
in glasses or individual glass dishes
with whipped cream spooned on top,
if desired. Decorate with mint leaves
or sprigs.
Yield: 6 portions.

Fruit lote

*This dessert is made throughout
Polynesia and in Fiji. The name,
recipe and flavor vary according to
country and cooking traditions, but
the final products are very similar.
Lote, poke, piasua, or hua as it is
known in Fiji, the Cook Islands,
Western Samoa, and Tonga
respectively, is served as a feast food.*

½ cup sugar
¾ cup raw grated manioc or
   4½ tablespoons minute tapioca
   or cornstarch
3 cups water
1 cup sliced banana
½ cup thinly sliced guava
½ cup diced papaya
1 cup diced pineapple
¼ cup lemon juice
1 cup thick coconut cream, or
   lighter alternative (page 6)

In a saucepan, mix sugar, manioc
and water. Stir well and bring to the
boil. Reduce heat, add prepared raw
fruit and simmer for 2–3 minutes.
Remove from heat and allow to cool.
Stir in lemon juice.
   Pour into serving dishes and chill.
Just before serving, top with thick
coconut cream.
Yield: 6 portions.

Note: If the mixture thins after

adding lemon juice, mix an extra
¼ cup grated manioc or 1 tablespoon
minute tapioca or cornstarch with
½ cup of mixture, stir into remainder
in saucepan and cook until thick.

Flaming fruit

*Raw ripe fruits such as mangoes,
pineapples and bananas may be
served in this way.*

Cut 1½–2 lb (600 g–800 g) fruit into
attractive, manageable cubes or
slices. Dip in sugar and then place
in a warm dish or chafing dish. Keep
in a warm oven until ready to serve.
Heat ½ cup brandy or rum in a ladle
over a flame and set alight. Pour
over the fruit. The flaming may be
done at the table where a candle can
be used to heat the spirit. Serve the

fruit while it's flaming — but with
care!

Variation: Peeled rambutans,
mangosteens and lychees can be
simply served in this way using a
liqueur with a high alcohol content,
such as Kirsch or Cointreau.

Pacific Islands fruit mousse

1½ cups fruit pulp or purée
   (mango, cooked papaya, crushed
   pineapple, mashed cherimoya or
   mashed banana)
6 tablespoons lemon juice
4 tablespoons sugar
1½ tablespoons gelatine
2 tablespoons water
2 cups cream or yogurt
2 egg whites, stiffly beaten

In a large bowl combine fruit, lemon

Fruit lote

Broiled fruit

½ medium pineapple
½ papaya
1 large mango
2 large bananas
2 large kiwifruit

Basting sauce:
2 tablespoons brandy
2 tablespoons honey
1 tablespoon lemon juice

Topping:
2 passionfruit
2½ cups whipped cream

Peel all fruits and cut into similar sized chunks or slices, about 1 inch (2.5 cm) thick. Thread fruit onto 8 skewers using variation of color. Mix basting sauce ingredients in a small bowl. Cut passionfruit and scoop out pulp. Fold in whipped cream. Set aside.

Brush fruit with basting sauce just prior to placing on rack in broiler. Broil for 10 minutes, turning and basting frequently. When done, the edges of fruit should be lightly browned. Serve immediately with the fruit-flavored whipped cream, or fruit purée sauce (page 74).

Lemon fruit custard

In this recipe, fruits are topped with a special lemon custard and toasted coconut or other nuts, to make an attractive and delicious dessert.

Sauce:
½ cup sugar
3 tablespoons cornstarch
1¼ cups water
¼ teaspoon salt
1 egg, beaten
1 tablespoon butter or margarine, melted
4 tablespoons lemon juice
½ teaspoon grated lemon rind

In a saucepan mix sugar, cornstarch, water and salt. Cook over a medium heat, stirring all the time, until the mixture comes to boiling point and is thick and smooth. In a separate bowl, slowly add some of the hot mixture to the beaten egg, stirring all the time. Return to the saucepan and cook over low heat for a minute

or so. Then stir in the butter, lemon juice and rind.

Fruit:
1 tablespoon lemon juice
1½ cups sliced banana
1½ cups cubed fresh pineapple
1½ cups cubed fresh papaya
toasted coconut or toasted chopped nuts
whipped cream

Mix lemon juice with banana and combine with other fruits. Put in a bowl or individual glass dishes. Pour over sauce and chill. Just before serving, sprinkle toasted coconut, or toasted chopped nuts such as macadamia or almonds, over the top. Alternatively, garnish first with a spoonful of whipped cream and then add chopped nuts or coconut.
Yield: 6 portions.

Microwave note: Mix first 4 ingredients in a 4-cup glass measure. Cook 2 minutes on high, stirring twice. Add egg as directed and cook 30 seconds. Stand 5 minutes and proceed as above.

Bananas with orange and nuts

6 large bananas
3 tablespoons butter
4 cardamom pods
2 teaspoons cornstarch
1 cup orange juice
2 tablespoons lemon juice
½ cup soft brown sugar
½ cup chopped, toasted nuts (macadamia, almond, pecan or hazelnut)

Peel the bananas and cut in half. Heat butter in a large frypan and gently fry the bananas until golden brown. Lift out and arrange in a serving dish. Add cardamom to butter and sauté for a minute or so. Mix cornstarch with fruit juices and brown sugar. Stir into butter and simmer until it begins to thicken. Pour over bananas. Serve topped with chopped toasted nuts.
Yield: 6 portions.

Note: A good dessert to serve with ice cream.

juice and sugar. Soften gelatine in water, add a little of the fruit mixture and melt in microwave or over heat. Combine melted gelatine with remaining mixture. Chill until half set. Fold in whipped cream and egg whites. Set in a mold or individual glass dishes. Garnish with a piece of the fresh fruit, a maraschino cherry or a spoonful of whipped cream. Delicious served with coconut fruit cookies (page 85).
Yield: 6 portions.

Variations: Combine base ingredients as follows: banana and soursop or guava purée; mango and orange; passion fruit and papaya; equal parts soursop purée and mashed avocado; papaya and brandy.

Fijian manioc (cassava) pudding (vakalavalava)

All the Pacific Island countries have their own cookery methods for making dessert-type dishes out of grated root crops and coconut cream. Grated coconut, pounded tree nuts and fruits, may also be included in the mixture. The flavor reflects the natural ingredients and little sugar is included. Traditionally, the pudding is wrapped in leaves and baked in the earth oven. Many recipes have now been adapted for cooking by modern methods. A typical example is vakalavalava.

2–3 tablespoons sugar
1½ cups medium coconut cream
2 ripe bananas, mashed
2 cups finely grated manioc root

Mix the sugar with the coconut cream, add the mashed banana and manioc. Put the mixture in a 9-inch (23-cm) baking dish. Bake at 350°F (180°C) for at least 1 hour. When cooked, the mixture in the center will puff up and the surface turn a rich brown color. Serve hot or cold with coconut cream.
Yield: 6 portions.

Variation: Replace the coconut cream with 2 cups of milk. The pudding resembles an old fashioned English milk pudding.

TROPICAL FRUITS

Tropical fruits like guava, passion fruit, pineapple, soursop and mango provide the basis for the most delicious ice creams and sorbets. These are easy to make and store well in the freezer. The sorbet, made from water, fruit and sugar, is a fat-free alternative to ice cream. It may be served as an appetizer or dessert at a formal dinner, and is always a popular snack for children. The smooth texture of ice cream depends on having a fairly large amount of sugar and fat in the recipe. One way to reduce the calories and improve flavor and nutrition, is to include fruit in the mixture. Here are some interesting ideas.

Fruit sorbets

1 teaspoon gelatine
1 cup water
1 cup sugar
2 cups fruit juice or purée
3 tablespoons lemon juice
1 egg white, stiffly beaten

Mix gelatine with ¼ of the water. Add remaining water to the sugar and heat until dissolved. Stir in gelatine and cool. Add fruit juice or purée and lemon juice, and freeze to a mush-like consistency. Beat well until smooth and then fold in beaten egg white. Freeze until firm.
Yield: 3 cups.

Note: Many sorbet recipes do not contain gelatine, but we believe it helps to retain a firmer consistency in hot climates.

Suggested juices or purées for sorbets

Guava
Make guava purée by rubbing cooked fruit through a strainer.

Mango
Blend or strain fresh or lightly cooked ripe mango.

Soursop
Peel a ripe fruit, remove seeds and make a purée by rubbing soft flesh through a strainer.

Passionfruit
Cut fruits in half and scoop out pulp. Strain to remove half or all the seeds. Omit lemon juice.

Papaya
Peel fruit, remove seeds, cut up and mash or blend to make a purée. Omit gelatine unless cooked.

Pineapple
Chop up finely prepared fruit and blend. Omit gelatine unless cooked.

Citrus
Orange, lemon or grapefruit juice make refreshing sorbets. Orange and grapefruit pulp may also be included.

Banana
Mash or blend with 2 tablespoons lemon juice.

Avocado
Mash or blend ripe fruit with 2 tablespoons lemon juice and ¼ teaspoon salt.

For an interesting new flavor, try combining 1 cup of soursop with mashed avocado. Flavor the purée with sugar and lemon juice to taste. For a more exotic ice cream, include a liqueur, port or brandy, using about 1 tablespoon to 1 cup of fruit mix.

Fruit ice cream

A refreshing and simple dessert can be made by mixing prepared raw or cooked fruit with a good commercial vanilla ice cream in the proportions of 3 cups of fruit mix to 4 cups of ice cream. (Medium-sized packs usually contain 1 liter — 4 cups.)
   Prepare the fruit by blending, mashing or chopping finely. Strain off surplus liquid to make a fairly thick mixture. Add sugar, lemon juice and other flavorings in sufficient amounts to develop the taste of the fruit. The mix should have quite a strong sweet and acid flavor. Freeze until little ice crystals form. Then remove, allow to soften slightly, beat until smooth and fold

in the chilled fruit. Put the mixture in a covered container and freeze. When half-frozen, beat with a wooden spoon.

Avocado ice dessert

The idea for this easy to make dessert comes from America where ice cream makers were quick to see that avocado was an ideal fruit for sweet and savory frozen dishes.

2 cups mashed or blended avocado
¼ cup honey
¼ teaspoon salt
¼ cup lemon or lime juice

Combine all ingredients in a blender or beat in a bowl. Pour into freezer trays and freeze. When half frozen, stir well. Serve in individual dishes, garnished with half a maraschino cherry, chopped toasted nuts or whipped cream.

Pineapple glacé

3 small pineapples
6 tablespoons sugar
6 tablespoons Cointreau
3 cups vanilla ice cream

Wash and rinse the whole pineapples thoroughly. Drain well. Keep the crowns (tops) intact and dry the pineapples with paper towel.

Cut each pineapple in half lengthwise, being careful not to break the leafy crowns from the fruit. Using a sharp knife remove most of the flesh leaving about a ½-inch (1.5-cm) thick shell. Set the flesh aside. Sprinkle the inside of each shell with 1 tablespoon each of sugar and Cointreau.

Cover loosely with plastic wrap and chill for 4 hours. Dice the pineapple flesh very finely, then quickly combine with ice cream, reserving some for garnish. Pile lightly into the 6 shells. Place each one in a plastic bag and freeze until firm, for about 2 hours. Remove from freezer, unwrap, garnish with a few chunks of pineapple and serve.
Yield: 6 portions.

Variation: To reduce the strong pineapple flavor, replace 3 small pineapples with 1 medium pineapple. Prepare in the same way but reduce sugar to 3 tablespoons.

Pineapple glacé

Pie pastry

Makes one 9-inch (23-cm) shell.

1¼ cups flour
½ teaspoon salt
½ cup chilled butter or margarine
3 tablespoons iced water

Sift flour and salt into a bowl. Cut in butter using pastry blender or two knives until mixture is crumbly. Do not cut too finely. Working quickly, sprinkle iced water over top, mix gently with a fork to form dough into a compact ball. Wrap in waxed paper and chill if room is above 80°F (26°C).

Roll dough into a circle, 1 inch (2 cm) larger than pie plate. Lift and fit into place, trim around rim by pinching. Fill and bake.

Note: Pastry should be eased, not stretched, into a pie plate. Stretching will cause the pastry to shrink when baked, resulting in a shell that is too small. In hot weather chill flour and mixing bowl.

For an unfilled baked shell, prick the entire pastry base, particularly in the crease, with a fork. Then bake at 450°F (230°C) for 12 minutes.

Banana orange pie

½ cup sugar
1½ tablespoons cornstarch
1 cup orange juice, fresh or frozen
1 tablespoon butter or margarine
3 oranges, peeled, cut into segments, white pith removed
1 tablespoon gelatine
2 tablespoons water
1 baked 9-inch (23-cm) pastry shell
4 medium bananas, diagonally sliced
whipped cream for garnish

In a medium-sized saucepan mix sugar and cornstarch, stir in orange juice, add butter or margarine. Cook over medium heat until thick and clear. Add half the orange segments. Soften gelatine in cold water then stir into thickened juice mixture until dissolved. Chill mixture until it thickens. Spoon mixture into baked pie shell. Arrange sliced bananas on top of the mixture, interleaving with orange segments. Refrigerate pie until well set. Serve garnished with whipped cream or ice cream.
Yield: 6 portions.

Microwave note: In a large glass measure mix sugar, cornstarch, juice and butter. Cook on high for 3 minutes, stirring at 1 minute intervals. Stir until smooth. Cook 30 seconds more to thicken. Stand 1 minute. Mix in softened gelatine until dissolved. Proceed as directed.

Sweet potato custard pie

pastry for 9-inch (23-cm) shell
2 eggs, well beaten
1 cup cooked and mashed sweet potato
½ cup brown sugar
½ teaspoon cinnamon
¼ teaspoon salt
¼ cup brandy or rum (optional)
1 tablespoon lemon juice
2 cups milk
extra ¼ cup brown sugar
extra ¼ teaspoon cinnamon

Line pie plate with pastry and trim edge. Beat eggs and blend in sweet potato, sugar, ½ teaspoon cinnamon, salt, brandy and lemon juice. Blend until smooth. Add milk and blend for 30 seconds. Pour into pie shell. Mix last two ingredients in a small bowl and sprinkle on top of custard.

Bake at 450°F (230°C) for 10 minutes. Reduce heat to 325°F (160°C) and continue baking for another 20–25 minutes or until an inserted knife comes out clean. Serve warm or cold, topped with whipped cream or ice cream.
Yield: 6 portions.

Mango pie

pastry for 9-inch (23-cm) shell
2 lb (1 kg) ripe mangoes
¼ cup lemon juice
1 cup water
¼ cup sugar
2 tablespoons cornstarch
1 tablespoon gelatine
2 tablespoons water
whipped cream

Peel mangoes and cut off flesh. Cut half the fruit into cubes and sprinkle with some of the lemon juice. Put remainder of the mango into a saucepan with water and sugar. Bring to the boil and simmer until soft. Rub through a sieve or strainer, or blend. Mix cornstarch with a little of the purée and stir into remainder. Return to heat and cook until thickened. Mix gelatine with water and stir into hot mango mixture. Add remaining lemon juice and stir well.

Arrange cubed mango in pie shell and pour over the hot purée. Chill and serve with whipped cream.
Yield: 6 portions.

Coconut pumpkin pie

pastry for 9-inch (23-cm) plate
3 eggs
¾ cup brown sugar
2 cups cooked or canned mashed pumpkin
½ teaspoon cinnamon
½ teaspoon nutmeg
½ teaspoon ground ginger
¼ teaspoon ground cloves
¼ teaspoon salt
2 cups milk
¾ cup grated coconut or 5 tablespoons desiccated coconut
1 tablespoon rum
whipped cream and toasted coconut shavings

Line 9-inch (23-cm) pie plate with pastry. Trim edge. In a bowl or blender beat the eggs, then add sugar and stir well. Add pumpkin, spices and salt. Gradually stir in milk until smooth. Fold in ½ cup coconut and rum. Pour into pastry shell, top with ¼ cup grated coconut, and bake at 450°F (230°C) for 10 minutes. Reduce heat to 350°F (180°C) and bake for a further 30 minutes or until an inserted knife comes out clean. Cool on wire rack. Serve at room temperature topped with whipped cream and toasted coconut.
Yield: 6 portions.

Opposite: Banana orange pie

Using ¼ cup batter for large crêpes, or half that amount for small crêpes, pour mixture into pan. Tilt to spread evenly. When top is dry and finely bubbled, flip and cook 1 minute more. Remove to rack, keep warm, covered with a towel, in a very low 200°F (90°C) oven until all crêpes are cooked.
Yield: 12 large or 24 small.

Lemon banana crêpes

12 basic dessert crêpes
1 cup whipped cream
1 cup mashed banana
l tablespoon lemon juice
2 tablespoons caster sugar
3 bananas peeled and sliced diagonally
6 thin slices or very thin wedges of lemon for garnish

Prepare required amount of crêpes. Whip cream and mix with mashed banana, lemon juice and sugar. Fold sliced bananas into mixture, reserving some for garnish. As crêpes come off the pan, spoon filling along the center and roll up. Place on serving plates, dust with sugar and garnish with slices of banana and lemon.
Yield: 6 portions.

Coconut chocolate crêpes

12 basic dessert crêpes
1 cup unsweetened whipping cream
1 tablespoon caster sugar
1 cup freshly grated coconut or ½ cup desiccated coconut
4 oz (125 g) semi-sweetened dark chocolate or chocolate chips
slivered toasted almonds for garnish

Prepare required amount of crêpes and keep warm. Whip cream, then mix in sugar and coconut. Spoon along the center of crêpe and roll up. Place two filled crêpes on each serving plate. Melt chocolate over low heat (or in microwave oven) and pour a little over each serving. Garnish with almonds. Serve immediately.
Yield: 6 portions.

Coconut chocolate crêpes

Basic dessert crêpes

1 cup flour
1 tablespoon sugar
pinch of salt
3 eggs
2 tablespoons melted butter or margarine
1½ cups milk

Sift flour, sugar and salt into a bowl. Beat eggs into dry ingredients with a wire whisk, one at a time, beating well after each addition. Combine butter and milk and slowly beat into mixture. Chill mixture for 1–2 hours. Lightly oil a crêpe pan or cast-iron frypan, and preheat over a high heat.

Meringues with crème de menthe filling

Petite tropical meringues

4 egg whites
1¾ cups sugar
2 teaspoons lemon juice
2 tablespoons boiling water

Put egg whites, sugar and lemon juice in a mixing bowl and stir well. Let stand 1 hour, stirring occasionally (sugar will partially dissolve). Place bowl in pan of hot water and beat until mixture becomes frothy, then add boiling water while beating at high speed.

Continue beating until mixture holds very stiff peaks. Lightly oil a large baking sheet. Drop well-spaced teaspoonfuls of meringue on baking sheet and bake at 200°F (100°C) until meringues are dry and lift off easily, about 1–1½ hours. Store in airtight containers until ready to use.
Yield: 36.

Meringue filling

1 cup whipped cream
1 tablespoon sugar
1½ tablespoons passionfruit juice
 or 1 tablespoon crème de menthe

Whip cream with sugar and flavoring until stiff. Sandwich the meringues together with whipped cream.

Pavlova cake

Make meringue mixture. Lightly oil a large sheet of waxed paper or baking parchment and place on baking sheet. Mark a 9-inch (23-cm) diameter ring on paper. Fill circle with meringue to an even 1½-inch (4-cm) wide x 1-inch (2.5-cm) deep ring around the edge. Bake for 2½–3 hours at 200°F (100°C). When cooked and cooled, transfer carefully to flat cake plate and fill with one of the following fillings:

1. Vanilla-flavored whipped cream topped with carefully cut pieces or slices of tropical fresh fruit such as kiwifruit, pineapple or mango.
2. Prepare 2 cups vanilla-flavored whipped cream and fold in 1 cup of finely chopped crystallized ginger. Decorate top with thin slices of crystallized ginger.
3. Prepare 2 cups whipped cream flavored with 2 tablespoons Tia Maria liqueur or dark rum. Fill pavlova shell and sprinkle the top with chocolate chips.

CAKES
BREADS, COOKIES & MUFFINS

TROPICAL BAKING

Baking in hot humid climates requires very careful storage of ingredients. Baking powder and dried yeast are best kept in airtight containers in a cool cupboard or refrigerator.

Keep sugar in a closed container to prevent moisture absorption. Flour must be fresh and also stored in a closed container so that it is free from moisture. Some kinds of flour bought in tropical countries need to be sifted before use.

Cake mixtures containing butter or margarine can appear very moist in hot weather and cooks may be tempted to add extra flour. However, the moisture is due to fat softening in the heat and extra flour could spoil the recipe.

CAKES

Tropical gâteau

Making a spectacular gâteau is not as difficult as it may seem but it does require following definite procedures.

Sponge base
A variety of sponges may be used but these should all have a light texture. The following bases would be suitable: angel, Genoese or light butter sponge. Flavor them with the juice or essence of the fruit being used. The layers of sponge must be the same thickness as the fruit and cream filling. To reduce cost and calories, use a high proportion of fruit to cream, or use reduced fat cream.

Always have three layers of sponge. As the gâteau is built up,

see that layers remain flat. The top must not have a dome shape. If this develops, trim off or turn upside down. Ensure that the whipped cream is slightly sweetened. Add a little liqueur to enhance flavor and to improve the keeping qualities of the cream.

Basic gâteau

2 sponge layers, 8–9 inch diameter (20–23cm) home-made or bought
2 cups heavy whipping cream
3 tablespoons icing sugar
1 tablespoon liqueur
2 cups fresh fruit, sliced or diced

Using a very sharp long knife with a serrated edge, split the sponge layers in half horizontally and slice off any risen top from top layers. Whip the cream, then stir in sugar and liqueur. Prepare the fruit. Select the best pieces for decorating the top. Place bottom sponge layer on flat serving plate. Cover with an even layer of fruit, leaving a 1-inch (2-cm) border at edge. Cover the fruit generously with flavored whipped cream. Carefully place next sponge layer on top. Repeat process to final layer of sponge and ensure that this is level. Then proceed to cover top and sides with remainder of whipped cream and decorate with fruit pieces. Chill until ready to serve.
Yield: 6 portions.

Banana, pineapple and rum cream gâteau

Bake banana bread (page 83) in two layer pans. Cool thoroughly and slice horizontally as in basic gâteau. Peel and cut 3 or 4 bananas in thick

slices and soak for 5 minutes in lemon juice. Peel and cut one medium pineapple (save crown for decorating) into similar sized pieces. Cut some pieces fin-shaped for top layer. Use whipped cream as directed in the basic gâteau and flavor with 2 teaspoons dark rum to each cup of cream.

Assemble the gâteau as directed in basic gâteau but use less whipped cream between layers. The pieces of fruit to be used on top may be soaked in a mixture of 2 tablespoons lemon juice and 2 tablespoons rum. Drain juice from fruit and sprinkle it over top layer before decorating with pineapple crown and fruit pieces. Put some whipped cream in a rosette-tipped piping bag. Surround the fruit with cream rosettes. Decorate the base with fresh flowers.
Yield: 8–12 portions.

Tropical fresh fruit cake

This simple recipe turns into a moist cake with a delicious flavor.

2 tablespoons butter or margarine
½ cup flaked or finely chopped nuts
¼ cup crystallised tropical fruit
2 bananas
½ cup orange juice
2 tablespoons honey
2 eggs separated
1 cup chopped fresh pineapple
¾ cup mixed dried fruit
1½ cups wholewheat flour
2 teaspoons baking powder

Grease a 8-inch (20-cm) cake tin with butter, using sufficient to allow nuts to stick to the sides and base. Sprinkle with nuts. Wash the sugar off crystallised fruits, slice thinly and arrange amongst nuts on base of tin.

Purée the bananas with orange

Banana, pineapple and rum cream gâteau

juice, honey and egg yolks, then add pineapple and dried fruit. Sift flour with baking powder. Mix fruit into flour, and lastly fold beaten egg whites into mixture. Carefully pour into greased cake tin. Bake at 350°F (180°C) for about 1 hour. When cooked, the cake will begin to shrink from the side of the tin and will turn a rich brown colour. Turn upside down on a wire rack. Serve fruit side up.

and beat until smooth. Flavor with rum and vanilla essence. Frost between layers and on top and sides of cake.

Yield: 8–12 portions.

Variation: Replace ½ cocoa with ¼ cup cocoa and 1 teaspoon instant coffee dissolved in a little milk.

Lolo coconut cake

2 eggs
1 cup white or brown sugar
1 teaspoon vanilla essence
1 cup flour
1 teaspoon baking powder
¼ teaspoon salt
½ cup thick coconut cream (page 6)

Topping:
Mix together:
3 tablespoons butter or margarine, melted
¼ cup brown sugar
1 cup freshly grated coconut
   or ¾ cup desiccated coconut

Beat eggs until frothy and pale. Gradually add sugar, beating continually until mixture is thick and light. Add vanilla essence. Sift together flour, baking powder and salt. Add one-third at a time to batter, mixing well after each addition. Heat coconut cream to just below boiling point, then fold into batter, mixing well.

Rum chocolate cake

Rum chocolate cake

½ cup cocoa
½ cup water
1½ teaspoons baking soda
½ cup butter or margarine
1¾ cups sugar
2 eggs
1 teaspoon vanilla essence
2 cups flour
½ cup cornstarch
½ teaspoon salt
1 cup sour milk (see note)

Note: Make your own sour milk by adding 2 teaspoons of white vinegar to 1 cup of fresh milk.

In a small saucepan, mix first 3 ingredients and cook over low heat, stirring until a smooth paste has formed. Remove from heat and allow to cool. Cream butter and sugar until light and fluffy. Beat in eggs and vanilla essence. Sift flour, cornstarch and salt together, and add to batter alternately with sour milk, beating well after each addition. Pour into 2 well-greased round 9-inch (23-cm) cake tins and bake at 350°F (180°C) for 30–35 minutes. Leave in tin 5 minutes then remove and cool on racks. Frost with the following:

Chocolate rum frosting

2 cups icing sugar
½ cup cocoa
1 egg, beaten
¼ cup softened butter
¼ cup milk
2 teaspoons dark rum
½ teaspoon vanilla essence

Sift sugar and cocoa into a bowl. Beat in egg and butter. Add milk

Lolo coconut cake

Pour into well-greased 9-inch (23-cm) cake tin and bake at 350°F (180°C) for 30–35 minutes or until golden brown and springy to the touch. While cake is cooking, mix topping ingredients together. Remove cake from oven and spread with topping mixture. Return to oven using broiler heat only. Watch carefully to prevent burning while broiling 3–4 minutes until toasted a rich golden color. Cool cake in pan. **Yield**: 8–12 portions.

Microwave note: Pour batter into glass tube pan, or glass casserole with glass in centre. Bake on medium for 2 minutes, ¼ turn, bake 2 minutes, ¼ turn, bake 2 minutes. Check for evenness of cooking. Stand 5 minutes. Add topping to cake and broil in oven.

Variations: 1. ½ cup canned coconut cream can replace fresh coconut cream, resulting in a very light-textured cake.
2. Use ½ cup piña colada plus 1 teaspoon butter to replace coconut cream. This cake is a little sweeter with a hint of pineapple flavor.

BREADS

Ripe breadfruit bread

This has a moist texture and a delicious, unique flavor.

½ cup butter or margarine
1½ cups sugar
½ teaspoon vanilla essence
2 eggs
2 cups flour
1 teaspoon baking powder
1 teaspoon baking soda
¼ cup milk
1 cup cooked mashed ripe breadfruit pulp
½ cup sliced crystallized ginger

In a bowl beat the butter and sugar until creamy. Add vanilla essence and beat in the eggs, one at a time. Sift in flour and baking powder. Mix baking soda with milk and add to the mixture with the breadfruit. Stir well and put mixture in a well-greased tin and decorate the top of

Ripe breadfruit bread

the cake with slices of crystallized ginger. Bake for about 45 minutes at 325°F (160°C) or until cooked. **Yield**: 8–12 portions.

Pumpkin or banana bread

½ cup butter or margarine
½ cup sugar
2 eggs
1 teaspoon vanilla essence
1½ cups flour
2½ teaspoons baking powder
½ teaspoon salt
2 tablespoons milk
1 cup pumpkin purée or 3 small or 2 large bananas, well mashed

Cream fat with sugar until light and creamy. Thoroughly beat in eggs one at a time. Add vanilla essence. Sift flour, baking powder and salt together. Alternately stir in dry ingredients and milk. Fold in

pumpkin purée or well mashed bananas. Pour into a well-greased 8-inch (20-cm) cake tin.

Bake at 350°F (180 C) for 30–35 minutes. Cool 5 minutes, then remove from pan and cool completely on cooling rack.
Yield: 8–12 portions.

Variations: 1. For a moister bread, use 2 tablespoons sourmilk or buttermilk plus ¼ teaspoon baking soda, instead of milk.
2. If using pumpkin, add 2 teaspoons mixed spices or pumpkin pie spice.
3. Add one of the following: ¼ cup raisins, ¼ cup toasted sunflower seeds, ½ cup coconut.
4. Use a combination of ½ cup cooked mashed pumpkin and ½ cup mashed banana, adding 1 teaspoon cinnamon and a pinch of ground ginger.

Mango ginger butterflies

COOKIES

Mango ginger butterflies

The biscuit base for this delicious dessert is Scottish shortbread and it has many uses. It makes a crisp and firm shell for cheesecakes and cream pies, as well as biscuits and short-cake. The pastry can be flavored with ginger or grated orange or lemon rind.

Shortbread base or cookies

½ cup caster sugar
1 cup butter
2 teaspoons crushed fresh ginger
  root or ½ teaspoon ground ginger
2 cups flour
½ cup cornstarch
¼ teaspoon salt

Cream sugar and butter together until light and fluffy. Mix in ginger. Sift flour, cornstarch and salt and work into mixture, using a pastry blender or fork until well combined. Keep mixture cool while working. (In hot weather use a chilled bowl or place bowl in a pan of iced water.) Pat dough into a ball, wrap and chill for 30 minutes.

Roll dough to ½-inch (1.5-cm) thickness on a lightly floured board. Using a 4-inch (10-cm) diameter cookie cutter, cut out 12 cookies. Place on ungreased cookie sheet. Prick with a fork. With a knife score 6 cookies in half, but do not cut through the dough.

Bake at 450°F (230°C) for 5 minutes then reduce heat to 350°F (180°C) and bake about 25 minutes or until they are an even pale golden color and dry-looking. Remove and cool 5 minutes on pan before removing to a paper-covered flat surface. Store in an airtight container until needed.

Mango filling

½ cup whipping cream
2 teaspoons rum, brandy or
  passionfruit juice
1 cup mango, thinly sliced and
  lightly cooked in sugar syrup

Whip cream and flavoring together and put into rosette-tipped piping bag. Drain mango very well.

Cut the 6 scored cookies into halves. On the remaining 6 cookies place mango slices, then pipe edges with cream. On each, place 2 cookie halves, forming butterfly wings. Pipe with more whipped cream and decorate with further mango.
Yield: 6 cakes.

Variations: 1. Use 2 teaspoons grated orange rind instead of ginger. Flavor cream with orange-based liqueur and use sliced kiwifruit.
2. Flavor cream with Kirsch and use canned pineapple.

Nut bread

This recipe may be adapted to include any kind of chopped or grated nuts. For example macadamia, or almond or Pacific Island tree nuts, such as cooked and grated Tahitian chestnut.

2 cups flour
3 teaspoons baking powder
¼ teaspoon salt
1 cup finely chopped nuts
¼ cup sugar
1 cup milk
2 eggs, well beaten
2 tablespoons melted margarine
  or coconut cream

Sift flour, baking powder and salt together. Add nuts and sugar. Combine milk, eggs and margarine and stir carefully into dry ingredients. Turn into a greased loaf tin approximately 9 inch (25 cm) long. Bake at 350°F (180°C) for about 45 minutes. Cool and serve fresh.

Variations: Use half nuts and half dried fruits. Replace 1 cup flour with wholewheat flour. Substitute brown sugar for white.

Coconut fruit cookies

2 cups flour
3 teaspoons baking powder
½ teaspoon salt
¼ cup butter or margarine
¼ cup sugar (optional as dried
   fruit adds sweetness)
¾ cup dried fruit mix
1 egg, beaten
approx ¼ cup milk
1 cup freshly grated coconut or
   ¾ cup desiccated coconut

Sift flour, baking powder and salt.
Cut in butter until the mixture
resembles coarse meal. Mix in sugar
and dried fruit. Mix egg, milk and
coconut together. Add to batter and
mix quickly with a fork until all
flour is dampened and forms a ball.
Transfer to a lightly floured board.
Knead 6 times. Roll dough to ½-inch
(1.5-cm) thickness. Cut into 2-inch
(5-cm) rounds, squares or diamond
shapes. Place on a prepared baking
sheet and bake at 425°F (220°C) for
12–15 minutes.
Yield: 20–24 biscuits.

Passionfruit coconut
squares

Base:
1½ cups flour
½ teaspoon salt
2 tablespoons sugar (optional)
½ cup butter or margarine
½ cup passionfruit jelly or jam
   (page 88)

Topping:
2 eggs, beaten
¾ cup brown sugar
1 teaspoon vanilla essence
2 tablespoons flour
pinch of salt
1 teaspoon baking powder
1 cup grated coconut or ¾ cup
   desiccated coconut

Mix flour, salt and sugar together
and rub in butter until a fine crumb
mixture. Press into 8-inch (20-cm)
well-greased baking pan. Bake at
350°F (180°C) for 5 minutes. Remove
from oven and spread generously
with passionfruit jelly or jam.
Topping: In a mixing bowl beat
together the eggs, sugar, vanilla

essence, flour, salt and baking
powder until light. Stir in coconut.
Pour over the jelly and spread
evenly. Return pan to oven and bake
for 20–25 minutes until top is golden
brown and springs back to the
touch. Cool and cut into 2-inch (5-cm)
squares.
Yield: 16 squares.

Variation: Use fruit salad jam
instead of passionfruit jelly or jam.

Banana drops

2 cups flour
¼ cup sugar
3 teaspoons baking powder
½ teaspoon salt
½ cup banana, mashed
1 egg, beaten
2 tablespoons melted butter or
   vegetable oil
2 tablespoons milk

Sift together flour, sugar and baking
powder and form a hollow in centre.
Mix remaining ingredients together
in another bowl, then pour into dry
ingredients and stir with a fork just
until all flour is dampened. Do not
over-stir. Drop by spoonfuls on to a
prepared baking sheet. Bake at
400°F (200°C) for 12-15 minutes.
Yield: 16–18 small biscuits.

Fresh fruit muffins and banana drops

Pumpkin scones (biscuits)

½ cup sugar
1 tablespoon butter or margarine
1 tablespoon hot water or strong
   coffee (optional)
1 egg
1 cup cooked or canned pumpkin
2 cups flour
3 teaspoons baking powder
½ teaspoon salt
½ teaspoon ground cinnamon
½ teaspoon freshly ground nutmeg

Beat sugar, butter and water. Then
beat in egg and pumpkin. Sift in
remaining dry ingredients and stir
with a fork just until all flour is
dampened. Do not over-mix. Drop
spoonfuls on to a prepared baking
sheet. Bake at 400°F (200°C) for
12–15 minutes.
Yield: 16 small biscuits.

MUFFINS

*Every cook looks for that 'never fail'
recipe which can be varied to suit
available supplies. Fruit muffins
provide the answer. The mixture is
easy to prepare and bake, and almost
any fruit may be included to provide
a different flavor.*

Spicy health muffins

½ cup crushed and well drained
   fresh or canned pineapple
1 cup grated carrot
2 tablespoons lemon juice
½ cup brown sugar
¼ cup melted butter or margarine
½ cup milk
1 egg, beaten
1 teaspoon baking soda
1 cup white flour
¾ cup wholewheat flour
2 teaspoons baking powder
2 teaspoons ground cinnamon

Mix together pineapple, carrot,
lemon juice, sugar, butter, milk and
egg. Mix baking soda with little of
mixture, then add to remainder and
stir well. Sift together flours, baking
powder and cinnamon, returning
bran to flour. Stir dry ingredients
into fruit mixture. Fill muffin tins
¾ full and bake at 350°F (180°C).

Yield: 9 large or 12 medium muffins.

Variation: Add ¼ cup chopped
crystallised ginger.

Fresh fruit muffins

1 cup flour
1 cup wholewheat flour
2 teaspoons baking powder
1 teaspoon baking soda
½ teaspoon ground cinnamon
¼ teaspoon ground nutmeg
¼ teaspoon salt
1 cup natural unsweetened yogurt
   or 1 cup milk and 2 tablespoons
   lemon juice
½ cup honey or golden syrup
¼ cup oil or coconut cream
1 egg, beaten
1 cup diced fruit (banana, ripe
   de-seeded guava flesh, pineapple
   or mango, well drained)

Sift first 7 ingredients together. In
another bowl mix yogurt, honey, oil
and beaten egg. Mix into dry
ingredients, and then fold fruit into
mixture. Fill prepared muffin tins
¾ full. Bake for about 20 minutes at
350°F (180°C).
Yield: 12 large muffins.

Jams, jellies, pickles and chutneys

JAMS, JELLIES, PICKLES & CHUTNEYS

Many of the tropical fruits and vegetables make wonderful jellies, jams, chutneys, pickles and relishes. The brilliant colors and different flavors of these preserves will enhance any repast. A home-made preserve adds a personal touch to a meal.

Simple curries served with freshly made chutneys become exotic dishes, whilst hot biscuits topped with guava jelly could provide the center of attention at a brunch or mid-morning coffee party.

In this section there are many simple and reliable recipes which use the fruits and vegetables commonly available in the tropics and now often found on the shelves of supermarkets throughout the world. The methods used in preparing these new foods are similar to those used for temperate fruits and vegetables. However, in hot climates and centrally heated homes, greater care must be taken when packing and sealing jars for long storage. Detailed information should always be sought from a reliable food preservation manual.

Included are some tropical pickles made from fresh fruits and vegetables suitable for immediate use, while others may be kept for a limited time in a refrigerator. In addition, there are also some interesting new ideas for stocking the store cupboard with longer-keeping pickles and chutneys.

Instructions for long-term storage of preserves in hot climates.

Thoroughly clean jars and then sterilize by submerging in water and boiling for 15 minutes; alternatively, place in an oven at 250°F (120°C) for 20 minutes.

For reliable long storage, use vacuum seal jars with sealing lids and screw rings. Boil the lids for 15 minutes. Pour boiling mixture into hot jars and immediately seal with lids. Screw lid firmly onto tops. Turn jars upside down and leave until cold. The tops of correctly sealed jars will dip in the middle, indicating that a vacuum seal has formed. Always store preserves in a cool, airy cupboard. Check often to see that dust and mold do not collect on jars.

Jellies

Brilliant, shimmering jellies made from tropical fruits are well worth the effort. Particularly suitable are fruits such as guava, passionfruit, rosella, kiwifruit, mango, Tahitian apple, Java cherry (lovi lovi), Brazil cherry and citrus.

Much of the quality and set of a jelly depends on the natural acid and pectin content of the fruit base. The first four fruits listed above are low in acid and therefore require the addition of lemon juice as an aid to setting. The other fruits are high in acid and do not need lemon juice. White sugar is preferable in jelly making as it does not alter the natural clarity and brilliance of the fruit juice.

As a rough guide, 1 lb (400 g) of prepared fruit will yield 1 cup of extracted juice. A juice extraction bag can be made from a 20-inch (50-cm) square of cheesecloth tied with strong cord.

Fruit preparation

Choose well-formed, slightly under-ripe fruit. Wash and remove stems, blossoms, blemishes and bruised parts. Large fruits should be cut into pieces. Put unpeeled fruit, including seeds, into a large pot and add sufficient water to just cover. Bring to the boil and cook until fruit is soft and mushy, stirring occasionally with a wooden spoon.

Passionfruit jelly requires an extra step. Cut fruits in half, remove pulp and set aside. Cut up skins and put in a pot and just cover with water. Boil gently for 30 minutes then drain water from skins and add to pulp. Discard skins and boil pulp for a few minutes.

Juice extraction

Drape a dampened cheesecloth in a large bowl then put in the cooked fruit and juices. Gather edges of cloth together to form a bag and tie off securely. Suspend the dripping bag several inches above the bowl.

For a clear extraction, allow the bag to drip untouched for several hours or overnight. Measure the quantity of extracted juice. Discard the pulp.

Measuring jelly ingredients

Successful jellies are a result of balanced amounts of juice to sugar. To every 1 cup of extracted juice from high-acid fruits, like Tahitian apple, Brazil cherry, Indian cherry, lime, lemon, orange, kumquat, green mango and passionfruit, add 1 cup sugar. To every ¾ cupful of extracted juice from low-acid fruits, like

rosella and guava, add ¼ cup lemon juice and 1 cup sugar.

Basic steps in jelly making

1. In a large pot, put a measured quantity of juice, sugar, and lemon juice if required. A total of 6 cups juice and 6 cups sugar per batch is a manageable amount.
2. Place the pot over medium heat and stir to dissolve the sugar.
3. Boil rapidly for approximately 15–18 minutes. Skim off foam as it forms during boiling, as it leaves unattractive streaks in the cooled jelly.
4. Test for jellying stage for the next few minutes. Put several ice cubes on a saucer and cover with a sheet of plastic wrap. Drop a teaspoonful of hot jelly on to the sheet, wait 30 seconds. A skin should be visible when gently pushed. This indicates jelly is ready to be poured into hot sterilized jars.

Note: Consult local food authorities and government publications for adjustments to temperatures and cooking times at altitudes above 1000 feet (300 meters).

Jellies and their uses

Brazil cherry jelly is a pinkish yellow color with a sharp flavor. Delicious spread on biscuits or hot breads. Provides a tart accompaniment for meats.

Java cherry (lovi lovi) makes a deep red shimmering jelly with an acid flavor. Very good as a spread or served with meats.

Guava jelly is a deep pink and has a unique flavor. It is particularly suited as a spread or cake filling.

Tahitian apple jelly is pale pink and very similar to apple jelly in flavor.

Passionfruit gives a golden jelly with a sweet, fairly bland flavor. It makes a good spread.

Mango jelly is amber-colored and makes a delicious spread.

JAMS & MARMALADES

Fruit preparation

Fruits should be fully formed and slightly under-ripe. All blemishes and bruises must be cut away, seeds and pips removed, and large fruits peeled and chopped. Retain all juice with chopped fruit.

Measuring jam ingredients

Good quality jams are a result of correct amounts of fruit pulp and sugar. Low-acid fruits need added lemon juice. High-acid fruits may be combined with sugar at a one-to-one ratio. During boiling, stir occasionally to prevent fruit sticking to the pot. One pound (400 g) prepared fruit plus sugar and water will yield just over 3 cups jam.

Basic steps in jam making

Follow steps 1–4 in basic jelly making (page 88). At the setting stage, a spoonful of cooled jam will hold its shape. Ladle hot jam into hot sterilized jars and seal as directed for jelly. Jam is ready to use after standing 24 hours. It is quick to make, uses small quantities of fruit and is ideal for a gourmet gift with a personal touch.

Fruit salad jam

8 Tahitian apples
water
1 orange
2 cups cubed banana
2 cups cubed pineapple
2 cups cubed papaya
½ cup passionfruit pulp
2 tablespoons lemon juice
sugar

Wash and slice unpeeled apples. Put into pot and just cover with water. Boil until soft. Strain juice from pulp through a cloth. Put the juice in a large pot. Grate the rind from the orange and add to juice. Squeeze orange and add juice along with chopped fruit, passionfruit pulp and

Citrus marmalade and mango jelly

lemon juice. Bring to the boil and cook for 5 minutes.

Remove from heat and measure mixture. For every cup of mixture, add 1 cup sugar. Mix together in pot and bring to the boil. Continue boiling until mixture reaches setting stage (page 88). Follow sealing instructions (page 88).
Yield: 10–12 cups.

Note: Unripe mangoes or green apples may replace Tahitian apples. Peel and remove pips, then proceed as directed.

Citrus marmalade

1 large grapefruit
2 oranges
8 kumquats
4 limes
sugar
water

Cut grapefruit and oranges into quarters. Remove seeds and center pith and slice very thinly, crosswise. Cut kumquats in half and remove all seeds, then slice into thin slivers. Retain all juices of fruit when cutting. Peel limes and discard skins. Cut flesh into quarters and slice thinly.

Combine all prepared fruit in a large bowl and just cover with water. Cover with a cloth and let stand for a minimum of 12 hours. Transfer mixture to a large pot and boil until rinds are tender. Cool and then measure. For every 1 cup of cooked pulp, add ½ cup water. Add 1 cup sugar for each cup of pulp and water.

For a tart marmalade, replace half the water with lemon juice. Mix well in pot and bring to the boil. Continue boiling until mixture reaches setting stage. Follow instructions for sealing or vacuum sealing (page 88).
Yield: 5–6 cups.

Note: The soaked rind mixture must be cooked until tender before sugar is added to avoid tough rubbery marmalade. For a solid fruit marmalade, reduce added water to ¼ cup.

Guava jam

4 lb (1.8 kg) slightly under-ripe
  guavas
water
sugar
lemon juice

Wash and cut guavas and put into large pot with enough water to barely cover. Boil until soft and then rub through a coarse sieve. Measure the pulp and juice mixture. For every ¾ cup of mixture add ¼ cup lemon juice and 1 cup of sugar. Put into a large pot and stir continually to dissolve sugar while bringing to the boil. Boil until mixture reaches setting stage, approximately 18–20 minutes. Test and follow instructions for sealing (page 88).
Yield: 10–12 cups.

Variation: Peel firm, pale yellow guavas. Cut in half and scoop out seeds and pulp with a spoon. Reserve the fleshy shell. Put pulp and skins in a pot. Cover with water and boil until soft. Strain through a cloth or sieve. Cut guava shells into strips or squares. Add to juice and boil until just soft. Measure in cups. Add 1 cup sugar and 1 tablespoon lemon juice to every cup of juice and fruit. Cook and seal.

SAUCES & PICKLES

Fruit ketchup

4 lb (1.8 kg) green mangoes,
  half-ripe guavas or tomatoes
water
1 large onion, chopped
1 cup sugar
1 cup white vinegar
1 tablespoon salt
1 tablespoon mixed spice (equal
  quantities ground nutmeg,
  cloves, ginger)
1 teaspoon ground cinnamon
4 clove buds
3 cloves garlic, crushed
1 tablespoon crushed fresh ginger
  root
2–3 chilis, de-seeded and chopped
1 lemon or lime rind, grated

Prepare fruit as follows:
Mangoes: Peel and remove the pit. Cut the flesh into slices.
Guavas: Peel, cut in quarters.
Tomatoes: Wash, remove blemishes and cut into quarters.

Put mangoes or guavas in a large pot and just cover with water. For tomatoes, add 2 cups of water. Cook the fruit and chopped onion until soft and then blend or sieve to form a thick purée.

Tomatoes and guavas must be sieved to remove seeds. Place the purée in a heavy saucepan and add the remaining ingredients. Cook over low heat for about 30 minutes. Stir frequently to avoid burning, adding extra water if too thick. Pour into hot sterilized jars or bottles. Seal with sterilized lids or crown caps. If well sealed, this sauce will last for 6 months. It may also be frozen.

Hot peanut tomato sauce

½ cup chilis
½ cup oil
1 clove garlic
1 tablespoon chopped parsley
½ cup peanut butter
6 medium tomatoes, peeled and
  chopped
salt and pepper

Wash, cut and de-seed chilis. Put in a jar and cover with oil. Close jar

with a lid and put aside for 3–4 days. Drain the chilis, reserving the oil. Put chilis in a mortar with the garlic and crush to a fine paste. Alternatively, use a blender. Add remaining ingredients and oil. Purée or blend to yield a thick sauce. Pour into clean jars, cover, and refrigerate.

Serve with steak, kebabs, and rice dishes.
Yield: 2 cups.

Fresh tomato sauce

1 medium onion, chopped
1½ tablespoons vegetable oil
1 cup peeled and chopped tomatoes
1 cup water or chicken stock
½ teaspoon sugar
½ teaspoon salt
1 teaspoon chopped fresh basil or
  ¼ teaspoon dried basil
2 teaspoons cornstarch (optional)
¼ cup water (optional)

Sauté onion in oil in saucepan. Add tomatoes, water, sugar and salt. Simmer for 10 minutes. Add basil and cook a few minutes more before serving. If a thicker sauce is desired, mix cornstarch and water and add to sauce. Cook until thick. Stored in a refrigerator the sauce will last for 2–3 days.
Yield: 2 cups.

Note: Substitutions for fresh tomatoes: equal amount canned tomatoes, or 2 tablespoons tomato paste plus 1 cup water, or ½ cup tomato purée plus ½ cup water**.**

Lime pickles

6 limes
6 tablespoons salt
3 teaspoons turmeric
approx 2 cups lime juice

Choose well formed, unblemished limes. Wash and cut lengthwise in quarters, almost to the base. Mix salt and turmeric together. Fill centers of limes with this mixture. Pack into sterile jars. Cover with lime juice. Cover with tight-fitting lids and set in warm place 80°F (50°C), preferably in the sun, for a week, shaking the jar once daily. Lime pickles are ready when rinds

are soft, which should be in 2 weeks.
Serve with fish, meat or vegetable curries. Store in cool cupboard or refrigerator.

Chili wine or vinegar

small hot chilis
fresh root ginger or whole dried root ginger
white vinegar, gin or dry sherry

Clean the chilis and remove stalks. Peel root ginger. Pack into bottles and then cover with vinegar, gin or dry sherry. Seal bottles and leave for several months. Use a few drops in soups, stews or tomato dishes.

CHUTNEYS

No curry is complete without serving at least two contrasting chutneys. Although there are some excellent commercial products available which adequately capture the spirit and taste of India, making your own is much more exciting. Here are some examples of easily produced chutneys — the variety is endless.

Hot spiced tomato chutney

2 tablespoons vegetable oil
½ teaspoon cumin seed
½ teaspoon fenugreek seed
½ teaspoon mustard seed
1 clove garlic, crushed
1 tablespoon crushed fresh ginger root
1 lb (400 g) tomatoes (fresh or canned), peeled and chopped
½ teaspoon turmeric
salt
1 teaspoon tamarind or lemon juice
1 tablespoon water
2 tablespoons coriander or chopped parsley

In a saucepan, heat oil and sauté spices for 2–3 minutes. Stir in garlic and ginger and cook another 2–3 minutes. Add tomatoes and turmeric and season with salt to taste. Mix tamarind to a paste with water. Add to tomatoes with coriander. Cook 10–12 minutes.
Pour into sterilized jars and cover

with lids. It is ready for serving immediately, or may be kept in refrigerator and used over 2–3 weeks.
Yield: 2½ cups.

Variation: Add 1 medium onion, chopped, along with garlic and ginger.

Microwave note: In casserole dish cook spices in oil on high for ½ minute. Add garlic and ginger, cook 1 minute. Add remaining ingredients, mix well and cook on medium for 5–7 minutes. Stand 5 minutes, covered. Proceed as directed before.

Mint chutney

2 cups whole washed mint leaves
1 tablespoon chilis, de-seeded and chopped
½ cup roughly chopped onion
1 clove garlic, chopped
1 large tomato, roughly chopped
salt and pepper
2 teaspoons soft brown sugar

Blend all ingredients until smooth. Adjust seasoning to taste. Refrigerate. Use same day.
Yield: 1 cup.

Chutneys

Mango chutney

5 lb (2 kg) mangoes, slightly
  under-ripe
¼ cup salt
8 cups water
3 tablespoons mixed pickling spice
3 tablespoons chopped fresh
  ginger root
4–5 small red chilis, de-seeded
2½ cups white vinegar
4 cups sugar

Peel mangoes, discard stones and
slice. Put into a large bowl. Thoroughly dissolve salt in water and
pour over sliced fruit. Let stand for a
minimum of 12 hours. Drain very
well. Put spice, ginger and chopped
chilis on a generous square of
cheesecloth, gather edges together
to form a bag, and tie off securely.
Put bag into vinegar in a large pot.
Add sugar and stir over heat until
dissolved. Then add mangoes. Bring
to the boil and simmer until mangoes
are just tender, but not mushy, and
partly transparent. The syrup
should be clear. Remove spice bag.
  Ladle hot mixture into hot sterilized jars, cap immediately and seal.
Yield: approx 6 cups.

Tamarind chutney

An essential chutney for curry.

1 lb (400 g) dried tamarind
4 cups cold water
1 clove garlic, crushed
1 tablespoon grated fresh ginger
  root
2 medium chilis, de-seeded and
  finely chopped
2 teaspoons mild curry powder
2 teaspoons turmeric
2 teaspoons soft brown sugar
salt
2 teaspoons black peppercorns,
  crushed

Soak tamarind in water for 2 hours.
By hand break up and squeeze the
tamarind in the water until a thick
juice is obtained, or rub through
strainer. Adjust water amount to
obtain 3 cups juice.
  In a heavy saucepan, gently fry
garlic, ginger and chilis. Add curry
powder and tumeric. Cook for 5
minutes. Take off heat and add

tamarind juice. Add sugar, salt and
peppercorns. Return to heat, cover
and cook very slowly for about 45
minutes, stirring frequently. Adjust
seasoning, cool and store in the
refrigerator in closed jars.
Yield: 3 cups.

Madras coconut chutney

1 cup roughly chopped onion
1 clove garlic, chopped
1 large ripe tomato, roughly
  chopped
1 tablespoon mild chili, de-seeded
  and chopped
¼ cup coriander or parsley leaves
2 cups freshly grated coconut
  (page 7)
salt

Blend onion, garlic, tomato, chili
and coriander until smooth. Add
coconut and salt and mix thoroughly.
Refrigerate but use within one day
of making.
Yield: 1½–2 cups.

Fresh tomato chutney

2 cups de-seeded and finely
  chopped firm tomatoes
2 cups finely diced onions
1 cup finely chopped coriander
  leaves or parsley
1 cup finely chopped green pepper
salt and freshly ground pepper

Prepare all ingredients and combine.
Chill and serve. Use same day.
Yield: 4–5 cups.

Hot pineapple chutney

5 lb (2 kg) pineapple, peeled
2 cups sugar
3 cups white vinegar
3 cloves garlic, crushed
1½–2 tablespoons chopped fresh
  ginger root
2 medium onions, chopped
2 teaspoons salt
1 lemon rind, grated
1 cinnamon stick
2 red chilis, de-seeded and
  chopped

Cut pineapple into small cubes. In a
large pot mix together all ingredients.
Bring to the boil, then reduce heat

and cook slowly until mixture has
thickened. Ladle hot chutney into
sterilized jars. Cool and seal.
  This chutney may also be frozen.
Yield: approx 5 cups.

Variations: Add ½ cup blanched
chopped almonds and 1 cup raisins
to mixture towards end of cooking
time.
  Substitute 1 lb (400 g) cubed, de-
seeded watermelon for 1 lb (400 g)
pineapple. The pink and yellow fruit
combination makes this a visually
attractive chutney.
Yield: approx 4 cups.

Pickled fruits

*A number of immature green fruits
or nuts make excellent pickles. A well
known delicacy is the pickled walnut.
The following recipe may also be
used for young eggplant, green
tomatoes, cucumber or watermelon.*

2 lb (800 g) of chosen fruit
¾ cup salt
4 cups water
1 large onion, sliced
2–3 cloves garlic, crushed
2 teaspoons yellow or black
  mustard seeds
2 teaspoons black peppercorns
4 cups vinegar
2–3 small chilis (optional)

Trim eggplant fruits and score skins
with a knife. Cut tomatoes and
cucumbers into slices. Make a brine
from salt and water. Add prepared
fruit and onion, and leave for 3
hours. Drain and rinse in cold water.
Combine spices with vinegar. Bring
to the boil and add fruits. Stir over
low heat for 2–3 minutes. Put into
sterile jars and seal.
Yield: approx 4 cups.

Variation: If using watermelon,
peel, remove seeds and cut flesh into
1-inch (3-cm) strips. Omit onion.
Add 1 stick cinnamon to spices. Boil
vinegar and spices. Cool and pour
over melon. Cover and seal.

ISLAND DRINKS

Before the arrival of western explorers, Pacific Island people obtained their drinks from the coconut and the clear streams. On special occasions a drink, commonly known as poi, was made by combining mashed ripe fruit, coconut water and cream.

Newcomers to the Islands soon found that all the popular fruits made excellent drinks. Today these are used to make a wide range of delicious and refreshing punches, cocktails and coolers. Because many party guests are now asking for non-alcoholic drinks, we have included a number of new and exotic recipes.

All cold drinks must be well chilled. Serve with ice or crushed ice and a garnish. Colorful garnishes include maraschino cherries, papaya, or melon balls, and pineapple segments served on toothpicks, or slices of lemon, orange or cucumber. Sprigs of mint, peppermint, lemon balm and blue borage, lemon or orange flowers, add to the flavor and color of the drink. An interesting alternative is to put pieces of fruit on a toothpick and then freeze in ice cubes, or freeze fruit in cubes to float on top of a bowl of punch.

The preparation of fruit-based drinks may be simplified by keeping on hand basic ingredients such as syrups, citric acid and frozen cubes of lemon or orange juice. Punches and coolers may be served in small glasses, allowing 4–5 fl.oz or ½ cup per person, as a pre-dinner drink or, for a party, in larger glass, ¾–1 cup (6–8 fl.oz) in size. Whenever possible, serve drinks in chilled glasses.

Basic syrup for drink

1 lemon rind
2 cups sugar
2 cups water
1 teaspoon citric acid

Sunset punch

Peel the lemon rind using a potato peeler or sharp knife. Put in a saucepan with the rest of the ingredients and bring to the boil. Simmer 5 minutes, strain, pour into hot sterile bottles, seal and store in a cool place.

Low calorie syrup

Replace all, or some, of the sugar with an artificial sweetener using instructions on container to judge the amount needed to replace 2 cups of sugar. For most brands 2 tablespoons sweetener = 1 cup sugar.

Acid flavour

All fruit drinks are improved by the addition of some acid flavour. Fresh lemon, lime or kumquat juice are the best ingredients. For a regular supply, freeze juice in ice cube trays and store in plastic bags. The acidity of 1 cup of lemon/lime/kumquat juice may be replaced by 1 teaspoon citric acid dissolved in 1 cup warm water.

Spicy flavours

Infusions made from spices, herbs and tea leaves provide an excellent subtle flavor to punches and long drinks.

Tea

Infuse 2 teaspoons tea in 1 cup boiling water. Leave 3–5 minutes and then strain through a cloth. Vary flavour by using a commercial spiced tea. Indian teas usually include cardamom, nutmeg, cloves and cinnamon. Alternatively, make your own spiced tea.

93

Spiced tea

4 cups water
2 teaspoons chopped fresh ginger
  root
8 whole cloves
2-inch (5-cm) cinnamon stick
8 teaspoons tea

Put the water and spices in a
saucepan and bring to the boil.
Simmer 5 minutes, then cool and
strain. Bring the spice liquid to the
boil, add tea, leave for 3–5 minutes
and strain through a cloth.

Variation: Omit tea and use spiced
liquid as base for drink.

Lemon leaf or grass tea

12 mature lemon leaves or 20
  blades lemon grass
4 cups water

Crush the leaves or grass by hand
and put into a saucepan of boiling
water. Cool and strain.

Variation: Add a small bunch of
fresh mint.

Pineapple tea

This simple and refreshing drink is
made from pineapple skin and
leftover trimmings. Put skins and
trimmings in a saucepan. Cover
with water and bring to the boil.
Simmer for 5–10 minutes. Add a few
lemon leaves to the liquid and leave
to cool. Strain and serve chilled.

Fruit tea punch

ice
1 bunch fresh mint
8 cups fresh tea or spiced tea
1 cup lemon juice
1 cup guava juice
2 cups pineapple juice
½ cup sugar syrup
1 whole lemon, sliced
1 cup cubed pineapple

Freeze large piece of ice in 1-quart
(1-liter) container. Crush the mint
and tie stems with piece of cotton.
Combine all ingredients and pour
over ice. Cover and leave for an hour
or so. Remove mint and add extra
ice cubes before serving.
Yield: 24 punch glasses.

Pineapple lime punch

2 cups guava jelly
2 cups boiling water
2 cups pineapple juice
1 cup orange juice
2 cups fresh lemon or lime juice
4 cups chilled ginger ale

Beat or blend jelly till frothy. Add
boiling water and stir till dissolved.
Add fruit juices and pour over large
piece of ice. Cover. Just before
serving stir in ginger ale.
Yield: Approximately 26–28 punch
glasses.

Mango papaya punch

1½ cups papaya juice
1½ cups mango juice
½ cup lemon juice
1 cup spiced tea
3 cups tea (page 93)
1 whole lemon or lime, sliced

Mix first 5 ingredients and chill.
Just before serving add sliced lemon
and ice cubes.
Yield: 15 punch glasses.

Sunset punch

*Beautiful to look at and refreshingly
delicious, this drink is ideal for any
festive occasion.*

3 lb (1.2 kg) watermelon
1 cup watermelon balls
2 cups watermelon juice
2 cups pineapple juice
¼ cup lemon juice
2–4 sprigs mint
4 cups chilled soda water
½ cup pineapple wedges
½ cup papaya or mango cubes
1 whole lime, sliced (for garnish)
ice cubes

Cut watermelon in half and scoop
out 1 cup of melon balls. With a
spoon scoop out remaining red flesh,
remove seeds and blend to make a
purée. Alternatively, rub through a
wire strainer. Strain out juice by
putting purée in a cheese cloth bag
or lining a big strainer with the
cloth. Mix all fruit juices together in
a bowl and add half the mint. Chill.

  Just before serving, add soda
water and half the fruit. Reserve

remaining fruit and mint for garnishing drinks. Serve in glasses
with ice cubes and garnish with
slices of lime.
Yield: 16–18 punch glasses.

Passionfruit cooler

1½ cups fresh passionfruit juice
½ cup orange juice
¼ cup lime or lemon juice
2–3 cups water or soda water
syrup
ice cubes
orange slices

Mix fruit juices. Add water or soda
water and syrup to taste. Serve with
ice cubes and an orange garnish.
Yield: Approximately 8–10 glasses.

Green coconut cooler

*This is the traditional cooling drink
of all Pacific Islanders.*

Select fully formed green nuts,
allowing one nut per person. With a
sharp heavy knife remove the husk
from the top and slice off the base so
that the nut stands upright. Cut off
the top of the nut or make two holes
through the 'eyes'. Chill and serve
with a straw. When finished, scoop
out the soft inner flesh with a spoon.
It's delicious!

Soursop cooler

*The unique flavour of this fruit lends
itself to making a very 'special'
tropical drink.*

3 cups soursop purée (page 74)
¼ cup lemon juice
3 cups water
syrup
sliced lime or watermelon balls,
  for garnish
ice cubes

Mix the soursop purée with lemon
juice and water. Add syrup to taste.
Serve garnished with lime slices or
watermelon balls and ice cubes.
Yield: 12 punch glasses

Variation: Replace water with
watermelon juice to make a pale
pink drink.

DRINKS WITH ALCOHOL

Malolo sunset cocktail

Fiji version of piña colada, inspired by the fruits of the Islands and amazing sunsets.

1 cup thick coconut cream (page 6)
1 cup canned mango juice
1½ tablespoons white rum
1½ tablespoons Mandarine
 Napoleon or Grand Marnier
1 cup ice cubes
peeled lime or orange skin
thin circles of coconut

Put coconut cream, mango juice, rum, Mandarine and ice in a blender. Blend well. Fill cocktail glasses with crushed ice and pour in cocktail mixture. Twirl orange or lime skin onto bamboo skewers and cap with a tropical blossom. Place a crescent of coconut on top of glasses.
Yield: 6 glasses 4 oz (125 ml) servings.

Mango cup

3 cups mango juice
¼ cup lime or lemon juice
1 teaspoon grated rind lemon or
 lime
½ cup brandy
1 x 26 oz (750 ml) bottle semi-
 sweet sparkling wine
ice cubes
maraschino cherries
mint leaves

Mix fruit juices, rind and brandy and chill. Just before serving add wine and ice cubes. Garnish with a cherry and mint leaf on a tooth pick.
Yield: 11–13 punch glasses.

Guava wine punch

1 cup guava juice
1 cup pineapple juice
1 cup lemon or lime juice
6 slices cucumber
1 whole orange, sliced
1 whole lemon or lime, sliced
sprigs mint
3 x 26 oz (750 ml) bottles dry
 white wine
ice cubes
syrup

In a punch bowl, mix fruit juices, cucumber, fruit slices and mint. Chill well. Just before serving add wine, ice cubes and syrup to taste.
Yield: 23–24 punch glasses.

Variation: Replace guava with extra pineapple juice.

Fiji rum punch

Sugar cane, grown in the western lands of Fiji, provides the natural ingredient for excellent rum. Fiji rum punch is an ideal party drink.

1 cup spiced tea
¾ cup lemon or lime juice
2 cups orange juice
1 whole lemon or lime sliced
1 x 26 oz (750 ml) bottle dark or
 light rum
1 bottle chilled ginger ale
1–2 cups sugar syrup
ice cubes

Mix all ingredients except ginger ale and ice, and chill for several hours. Just before serving, add ginger ale and ice cubes.
Yield: 20–24 punch glasses.

Variation: Add one vanilla bean to mixture before chilling.

Green coconut cooler

GLOSSARY

Boullion cube — concentrated fish, meat or vegetable stock.
Broil — to grill.
Canapé — small tasty biscuit or filled pastry served with drinks.
Cassis — blackcurrant liqueur
Chard — silver or green beet
Choux — light pastry-like, baked cases used for canapés and desserts.
Citric acid — crystal concentrate made from citrus juice.
Confectioners' sugar — icing sugar.
Cornstarch — cornflour.
Crème frâiche — cream fermented with buttermilk.
Crisco — commercial vegetable fat.
Crudités — small pieces, toast, biscuits or vegetables served with a dip.
Curry leaves (*tejpati*) — aromatic leaves used to flavor Indian dishes.
Dijon mustard — a French mustard.
Eggplant — aubergine, baigan.
Ghee — liquid butter made from heated cream.
Green onions — spring onions, scallions.
Ground meat — minced meat.
Karela — bitter melon.
Ketchup — hot sweet or sour sauce.
Kokoda — dish made from raw fish marinated in lemon juice.
Manioc — cassava, tapioka.
Miti — flavored coconut cream sauce.
Pak choi — type of Chinese cabbage.
Piña colada — pineapple flavored drink with coconut cream.
Plantain — cooking banana.
Ramekin — small baking dish for individual servings.
Rourou — taro leaves.
Salsa — sauce made from fresh vegetables.
Season — to flavor with salt, spices or herbs.
Sensopai — Japanese green leafy vegetable of specific flavor.
Sweat — to half cook at low temperature often with butter.
Tabasco — very hot chili sauce.
Vakasoso — filled or stuffed.
Worcestershire Sauce — traditional highly flavored English sauce, served with meats.

Index

A GUIDE TO
TROPICAL FRUIT & VEGETABLES
41 full color pictures. Information on selection, uses, storage and nutrition

The Nutritive Value of Commonly Used Tropical Fruits and Vegetables per 4 ounce (100g) prepared raw food

Nutrients Measure	Calories kcal	Protein g	Fat g	Carbohydrate g	Calcium mg	Iron mg	Vitamin A mg	Thiamin mg	Vitamin C mg
FRUITS									
Avocado	213	1.9	23	1	20	0.7	49	0.07	9
Banana	112	1.2	0.3	26	12	0.8	8	0.03	14
Carambola	28	0.3	0.4	7	8	1	160	0.05	38
Ripe fresh coconut	390	4	40	4	14	2.2	0	0.04	2
Green Coconut	77	1.4	3.6	10	42	1	0.04	0.04	6
Custard apple	74	1.4	0.6	16	17	0.3	5	0.05	43
Durian	138	2.5	1.6	28	20	0.9	2	0.27	37
Guava	21	0.7	0.5	4	10	0.2	73	0.03	240
Jack fruit	78	2.2	0.3	17	18	0.8	190	0.04	6
Kumquat	43	0.9	0.5	9.3	25	0.6	175	0.07	39
Lime	9	0.7	0.3	0.8	23	0.3	12	0.03	46
Lichi/Lychee	70	1.1	0.1	16	2	0.5	0	0.05	49
Longan	71	1	1.4	16	23	0.4	0	0.03	56
Mango	65	0.7	0.2	15	10	0.3	267	0.06	41
Mangosteen	13	0.6	1	1	7	1	0	0.03	4.2
Melon, Water	23	0.3	0.2	5	6	0.4	33	0.01	7
Papaya	50	0.5	0.1	12	24	0.7	118	0.03	73
Passionfruit	38	3	0.3	6	10	0.6	130	0.03	18
Pineapple	37	1	0.1	8	27	0.3	4	0.04	21
Pomelo	42	0.7	0	10	14	0.5	33	0.03	45
Rambutan	58	0.7	0.1	14	22	2.5	0	0.01	59
Roseapple	23	0.7	0.2	5	13	0.8	0	0.02	8
Sapodilla	82	0.4	0.8	18	16	2.3	22	0.01	7
Soursop	65	1.3	0.4	14	12	0.5	3	0.09	27
Tahitian Apple	46	0.2	0.1	12	56	0.3	34	0.05	36
Tangerine	35	0.9	0.2	8	42	0.3	100	0.07	30
VEGETABLES									
Bitter melon	19	0.8	0.1	4.5	26	2.3	18	0.06	57
Long Beans	36	2	0.1	4	50	1.4	36	0.08	—
Winged Beans	43	3.2	0.9	5	62	1.7	—	—	—
Red Chilis	116	6.3	1.4	24	86	3.6	1100	0.37	96
Eggplant	15	0.7	0.1	3	10	0.4	8	0.03	3
Chinese cabbage	18	2.3	0.1	2	192	1.9	323	0.06	40
Taro Leaves	29	4.8	0.8	1	216	2.7	744	0.15	90
Gourds	12	0.7	0.1	3	17	0.5	5	0.03	20
Okra	20	3.1	0.2	1	82	1	20	0.09	34
STARCHY ROOTS AND FRUITS									
Breadfruit	104	1.5	0.4	24	25	1	4	0.1	20
Sweet Potato	97	1.4	0.2	22	29	0.5	10-* 2000	0.09	24
Manioc (Cassava)	131	0.5	0.2	32	20	0.2	2	0.06	15
Plantain	124	0.9	0.2	30	18	0.6	30	0.15	11
Taro	107	1.1	0.1	26	32	0.5	7	0.03	15
Yam	129	1.4	0.1	31	5	0.6	80	0.08	21

Yellow coloured provide more Vitamin A

References : *The Pacific Islands Food Composition Tables*, South Pacific Commission, 1994. *Food Composition Tables, for Use in East Asia*, Food and Agricultural Organisation of the United Nations, 1972. NZ Institute for Crop & Food Research Ltd.

Modern transport now takes tropical fruits and vegetables to every part of the world. Exotic produce is to be found in supermarkets or fruit and vegetable shops in most large cities and towns.

The best quality produce is often found in shops which cater for people from tropical countries. Sometimes there are shops which specialize in importing foods from the South Pacific, Africa or the West Indies. Here the quality of foods and the variety available are likely to be very good. There are also some supermarkets which specialize in tropical foods.

Before shopping for your tropical fruits and vegetables, make sure that you know something about the food that you wish to try in your menu. Know how to choose good-quality items and have an idea as to how you will cook and serve them. If in doubt about trying out your family

on something new, buy small quantities and have a tasting session. Most people will agree that these new foods add an exciting difference to daily meals, but not all will necessarily be to everyone's taste.

Having decided on the foods you are going to buy, think how you will use them in your menu. Choose foods which will complement the main meat or fish dish. For example, if serving pork you might accompany this with sweet potatoes and Chinese cabbage, followed by a pineapple and pawpaw dessert. If fish is your choice, think of serving this with taro leaves cooked in coconut cream and some yam, garnish with pieces of fresh lime and have a tossed tomato salad. Follow this course with a crisp orange and banana pie.

This section of our book is designed to help you know about the foods which will make an exciting difference to your meals and at the same time improve the nutritional value of the menu.

Avocado

Tropical varieties have a green or purple skin. Fruits vary in size but some of the best flavored are about the size of an orange. A ripe fruit is soft inside, but feels firm when pressed gently with the fingers.

Store ripe fruit in a cool place or refrigerate. Keep hard fruits in a warm dark cupboard till soft. Sliced avocado may be dipped in lemon juice and frozen whole or as a purée. (Lemon juice prevents cut fruit from going brown.)

To use cut ripe fruit in half, remove stone and any brown tissue, score with the tip of a knife and season with salt, pepper, lemon juice or French dressing. Serve halves filled with seafood or other savory mixtures. Purée fresh and frozen fruit to make mayonnaise, soups, or ice cream. Avocado purée combines well with bananas and soursop to make desserts. Mash and season for sandwich fillings. Frozen fruit does not keep its shape and is best used as a purée.

Food value has a high fat content and is a fair source of vitamins.

Bananas

The best eating bananas are the Cavendish and the short Ladies' Fingers. Both types should be firm and yellow when eaten.

Store in a cool dry place, preferably hanging. Mature green bananas may be ripened by putting in a large bag and hanging in a warm place. Freeze ripe bananas whole to make a refreshing iced snack for children. Split bananas and dry in the sun. Make into jam.

To use peel or mash and eat as a dessert with cream. To prevent browning sprinkle with lemon juice. Use bananas in fruit desserts like ice cream, mousse, jelly, or as a pie filling. Use in milk shakes. Fry and serve with bacon. For savories, cut in sections, roll in bacon and grill.

Food value a carbohydrate food which also provides vitamin C and some minerals. Ripe mashed banana is easily digested and makes a good first food for infants.

Bell Pepper or Capsicum

About 4 inches (10 cm) long. They should have a fresh, shiny appearance and be bright green, yellow or red in color, depending on variety and degree of ripeness.
Store covered in a cool place, preferably in a refrigerator, to retain crispness. Under good storage conditions they will last a week.
To use chop or slice and use in all kinds of salads and vegetable dishes. Cut in half, remove seeds and stuff with a meat and vegetable mixture, bake and serve with a fresh tomato or cheese sauce. Add to all vegetable dishes. An important ingredient in Chinese vegetable recipes. The bright green or red flesh provides a useful garnish. Blanch sliced or cubed peppers in boiling water for 1 minute, cool and use to garnish vegetable dishes or cooked salads and add to spicy-flavored fruit salads. The colour and delicate flavour of bell pepper improves the appearance and taste of many dishes.
Food value a rich source of vitamins C and A.

Bitter Melon

This unusual gourd is also called Kerela, Balsam Pear, Balsam Apple and Bitter Gourd. The climbing plant produces rough-skinned fruits, 4 in (10 cm) to 1 ft (30 cm) long. The fruits have crisp-textured outer skin with a sour flavour, varying in colour from pale to dark green, and should be used before turning yellow.
Store on racks in a cool place or in covered container in refrigerator. Fruits will remain in good conditions for 2-3 days in open storage and for a week under refrigeration.
To use cut fruits in half and scoop out seeds and pith. Cut into small pieces and sauté with garlic, onion and spices, if desired. Parboil and sprinkle on salads or parboil prepared half-fruits and fill with a meat or vegetable mixture. Put halves together and steam or bake. Some people put salt on prepared fruits to remove the sour flavour, but in most Asian cooking this sourness is considered necessary.
Food value a fairly good source of Vitamins C and A.

Breadfruit

Should be fully formed, firm and pale yellow in color. Ripe fruit is soft and has a sweet flavor.
Store in water, or refrigerate to slow ripening. Mature fruit keeps 1-2 days in cool weather. Sun-dry thinly sliced fruits and store in airtight containers. Soak in water before cooking.
To use scrape or peel off the skin, cut in wedges, remove seeds and steam; or boil or bake whole in the skin. To bake, wash, puncture with skewer and cook in 350°F (180°C) oven for about 1 hour or until soft. Cut into wedges and serve with butter. Cook whole fruit over hot coals, turning frequently.
Use cooked grated breadfruit in bread recipes, fishcakes. Cut into cubes for salad, or cut 2-inch (5 cm) pieces and fry in hot oil to make excellent chips. Include ripe breadfruit in cake and dessert recipes.
Food value a good carbohydrate food which provides some vitamins and minerals.

Carambola

Also known as Star Apple. These shiny, five-sided fruits are about 2-3 inches (5-8 cm) long with a translucent pinkish yellow colour. The fruit has a thin skin and firm, juicy pulp of tart flavor.
Store in a cool place for a day or two or put in a plastic bag and refrigerate. Blend to pulp and freeze for use in fruit dishes and drinks.
To use cut up, add water and sugar and simmer till soft, then strain and chill the liquor to make a refreshing drink. Cut thin slices crosswise and gently poach for 30 seconds in a light sugar syrup. Use the slices as a garnish for desserts or gateaux, or add to fruit salad or other fruit-based desserts. Toss thin slices with salt and chili powder to make a chutney for curry. Use the juice or finely chopped pieces to give a refreshing acid flavor to fresh vegetable chutneys, fruit drinks and chicken dishes.
Food value a good source of Vitamin C.

Chilies

Come in many sizes, colors and shapes. They vary greatly in hotness from the mild sweet chili to the very hot small chili. Always choose fresh whole fruits.
Store chilies in a cool place. The fruits deteriorate rapidly and are best kept covered in a refrigerator. For long storage, dry in the sun or pickle in vinegar.
To use remove the seeds and then grind or chop finely. Take care not to allow cut chili to touch skin as it can cause irritation, particularly to the eyes and face. Add chili to curries and Mexican dishes. A very small amount will develop the flavor of soups and most savory dishes.
Food value all chilies contain large amounts of Vitamin C and A, but because these fruits are only used in small quantities they do not contribute greatly to the nutritional value of meals.

Chinese Cabbage

Pak Choi has bright green tender leaves with firm white stalks sometimes tinged with purple. Should be gathered and sold as a whole plant.
To store wash and put in plastic bags and keep in a cool place. Has a short life when harvested.
To use gently poach small leaves complete with stalks in a little water and butter for not more than 2 minutes. Otherwise separate leaves from stems of the larger leaves, cut stalks diagonally into strips and cook in boiling salted water for 1 minute and then add the chopped leaves. Delicious if a small quantity of sliced ginger is added to the liquid. One of the main components of Chinese stir-fried vegetable dishes. Use shredded young leaves in salad.
Food value a good source of Vitamins A and C. Also provides minerals and some protein.

Coconut

Mature nuts should have a brown fibrous shell and water inside. Green coconuts provide a refreshing drink.

Store coconuts on shelves in a dry place. Mature nuts will last for several weeks, and green nuts for about a week. Coconut cream, made from the squeezed flesh of mature nuts, freezes well.

To use tap the shell sharply with a heavy knife around the centre. This cracks the shell evenly. Save the water for making coconut cream, or to drink. Grate or cut the flesh out of the shells. Add a little water to cut flesh and grind in a food processor or add water to grated flesh, then put coconut mixture into cheesecloth and squeeze out the cream.

Toast grated coconut in the oven and use as a topping for desserts. Use freshly grated coconut in cakes, scones, bread, sweets, biscuits, vegetable curry, and to make chutney.

Food value a good source of fat and fibre plus some protein.

Cumquat (Kumquat)

This small citrus fruit is bright yellow to green in colour. It has a distinctive tart flavour. Cumquat trees bear several times a year and the fruits are valued for their many uses.

Store on racks in a cool place or in perforated plastic bags in the refrigerator. Fruits last in good condition for 3-5 days in open storage. Cumquats make good preserves, and the cooked fruit freezes well.

To use cumquats have a high pectin content and make good jams and marmalades. A few cumquats will greatly improve the flavour of an orange or grapefruit marmalade. Whole fruits make good sweet or acid pickles which go well with pork and ham. Cumquat juice makes a good addition to any fruit drink. The pure juice is very acid and may be used to make raw fish dishes in place of lemon juice.

Food value a good source of Vitamin C.

Custard Apple

This tropical fruit comes from South America and the West Indies and is widely grown in tropical countries. It is also known as sugar apple and bullock's heart. Large heart-shaped fruits hang from bushy trees. Fruits are a brownish red color and contain several large seeds which are interspersed in a cream-colored, sweet and slightly granular pulp.

Store on racks. Pick when mature but still firm. Separate pulp from the seeds and freeze.

To use peel the brown skin of soft ripe fruits. The fruit tends to fall into segments which are best eaten fresh. Pulp may be removed from seeds and used in ice creams and sorbets.

Food value a fair source of vitamin C.

Durian

Oval fruit weighing 2-3 kg (5-7 lbs) are borne on large trees. Each fruit is covered in sharp pointed spikes. When mature the fruit becomes soft and has an offensive smell. The soft sweet pulp which surrounds large seeds is highly relished by durian eaters.

Store on racks in a cool, airy location away from the house. The smell of ripening fruits is offensive to many people.

To use peel off the spikey skin and separate the soft white segments. These should be eaten fresh. Some people say the flavour resembles gorgonzola cheese. The large seeds are edible.

Food value a fair source of vitamin C. Also contains a little protein and fat.

Eggplant (Aubergine)

Fruits are many colors, ranging from white, pale green and pale mauve to dark purple. Size varies according to variety. For the paler colored varieties, choose small to medium fruits. Mature fruits may have a lot of seeds. The newer types of dark purple fruits have more flesh and fewer seeds. For all kinds, fruits should be firm, skin tender and the end soft.

Store on wire racks in a cool place or in a container in the refrigerator. Fruits keep fresh for several days. Cooked eggplant dishes freeze well.

To use eggplant, peel, slice or cube. Young fruits may be cooked with the skin on. Dip slices in flour or batter and fry, sauté and add to vegetable dishes.

Food value is low.

Guava

Choose firm fruit of a large size and greenish yellow color. Small fruits tend to have a higher proportion of seed pulp.

Store on wire racks in a cool place or in the refrigerator. Firm fruits keep for several days in cool weather. Lightly cooked prepared fruit may be frozen. Ripe fruit has a strong smell.

To use wash and eat as raw fruit. Peel, cut in half, scoop out seed pulp, slice shells and cook in a syrup for about five minutes. Flavor with lemon juice and serve as dessert or add to fruit salad. Boil the pulp and strain. Use the purée to make jam or include in ice cream and gelatin desserts. Make jelly from half-ripe fruit. Boil up skins and half-ripe fruit to make fruit juice. The flavor of guava is enhanced by adding a little lemon juice. A guava ketchup for meat is made by replacing the tomato with guava purée in tomato sauce recipes.

Food value one of the best sources of vitamin C. A good raw fruit for children.

Jack Fruit

This tree bears fruits weighing up to 70 lbs (28 kg), which hang from the trunk and branches. Fruits are a greenish yellow color. Fruits have tough skin with a rough surface. Green fruit has a firm flesh which exudes a sticky sap on cutting. When ripe, sweet segments may be pulled from the core.

Store on wire shelves till ready to use. Green fruits will keep for 1-2 weeks before ripening. Cut green fruits will ripen if put into a closed plastic bag.

To use the sticky sap from jack fruit makes preparation difficult. This problem can be reduced by oiling hands, knives and preparation surfaces. Green fruits are cut into cubes and steamed or sautéed with curry spices, onion and garlic before adding stock or water. Jack fruit has a mushroom-like flavor. It makes a delicious vegetable curry. The ripe segments may be used as a fresh fruit or included in raw fruit dishes.

Food value a fair source of carbohydrate, vitamins and minerals.

Kiwano

Also known as Horned or Jelly melon or African horned cucumber. When fully ripened kiwano is a golden orange color, the pulp turning dark green and sweetening in flavor. It has a subtle taste of banana and lime.

Store may be stored at room temperature. If picked when first yellow ripening appears, fruit will keep up to six months in good conditions.

To use slice into wedges or cut in half lengthwise and eat directly from the shell with a spoon, sweetening and chilling if preferred. The pulp may be squeezed into a bowl to use in desserts, with ice cream, seafood cocktails or in long drinks.

Limes

Generally small in size with a smooth, brilliant green skin and a special aroma. Some varieties are yellow in color.

Store on racks in a cool place. If carefully handled they will keep for at least 7-10 days. Freeze the fresh juice in ice trays and keep in bags.

To use squeeze and flavor sweet and savory dishes. Excellent with grilled fish and in an accompanying thickened sauce for fried chicken. Lime juice is an important ingredient of many marinades for meat, chicken and veal. It is the correct marinade for making Tahitian raw fish salad. Use in jams, jellies, marmalade and to make many kinds of spicy pickles. Lime juice, sometimes with the grated rind, is used to flavor ice creams, sorbets and cream fillings for cakes and pies.

Food value a fair source of vitamin C.

Longan

This is a large tree of Southeast Asian countries. It bears clusters of small fruits with a brownish skin which surrounds a pulp-covered seed. The pulp has a sweet refreshing flavour.

Store on racks for a few days; longer in refrigerator.

To use peel off skin and eat raw.

Food value quite a good source of vitamin C.

Long Bean (Yard Long Bean)

This tropical climbing legume produces beans 1 ft (30 cm) and more in length. Beans vary in color from dark to pale green and have a distinctive flavor. They are usually marketed in tied bunches.

Store in perforated plastic bags in a cool place, or in the refrigerator, where they will keep in good condition for 3-7 days.

To use trim off the top and stem ends. Arrange beans in a bunch of similar lengths, hold with left hand on a board and with right hand cut beans diagonally into slices with a sharp knife. Alternatively, cut into suitable lengths for cooking. Young thin beans may be cooked whole and then tied or plaited to make an attractive vegetable garnish. Long beans may be included in any mixed vegetable dish, or cooked, cooled and served as a salad. The flavour of beans is enhanced by a little basil, spring onion or green coriander.

Food value a fair source of vegetable protein, vitamins and minerals. A good family vegetable.

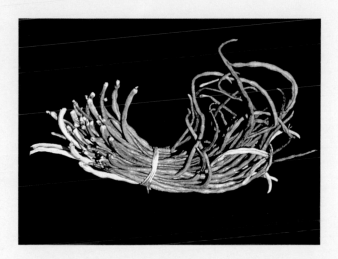

Lychee (Litchi)

The lychee comes from southern China and is now grown in most tropical countries. Bunches of pink, thin-shelled fruits hang from the branches of large trees. Inside the shell a pearl-grey, translucent fruit surrounds a seed. The fruit has a slightly chewy texture and delicious sweet flavour.

Store fresh for a day or two at room temperature in cool weather. Refrigerate for longer storage. The fruits are also dried, pickled and canned.

To use peel off the outer skin and eat fresh. The fruit pulp may also be used in salads, ice creams, sorbets and blended to make cold fruit drinks.

Food value quite a good source of vitamin C.

Mango

Can vary when ripe from those which are small and green to large reddish-yellow or green fruits. Avoid fruits with a stringy texture and turpentine smell. Good-quality fruits have a medium-sized seed and a sweet juicy yellow flesh, similar to a peach. Fruit should be firm and greenish to full yellow-red color, although some good varieties have a green skin even when ripe.

Store in a cool, dark place. Ripe fruit will not last more than two days. Peel ripe mangoes, slice and freeze.

To use cut the base off the fruit and peel downwards. Alternatively, slice off the sides of the fruit and press back skin and the flesh should come out easily. Use raw in fruit salads. Purée raw or cooked ripe fruit and use in ice cream, mousse and gelatin desserts.

Food value a very good source of vitamins C and A. Give mango juice to infants.

Mangosteen

This is a dark reddish purple fruit about the size of a small apple. The dark colored rind surrounds segments of juicy white pulp which adhere to seeds. This is the part eaten. Mangosteen is one of the most delicious of all tropical fruits. The rind contains a red dye which stains.

To use cross-cut the rind from stem to calyx and pull back from the fruit. The dark rind gives the appearance of flower petals which provide a background to the white juicy fruit. Alternatively, cut the rind round the middle of the fruit and scoop pulp out with a spoon. Best eaten raw. The pulp can be removed from seeds and blended to make a juice.

Store ripe fruits on racks in a cool place or refrigerate. Fruit is best eaten as soon as possible.

Food value This fruit's main advantage is its flavour. It has a low food value.

Manioc

(Cassava) Should be cream or light yellow in color. Blue-grey streaks in the flesh indicate that roots are not fresh. Roots should be crisp and break easily. Over-mature roots have a lot of hard fiber.

Store under cool damp conditions. Peeled manioc may be frozen raw.

To use peel, cut in 2½-inch (6-cm) pieces and steam or boil. You must discard cooking water. Use raw grated manioc in bread and biscuit recipes, to make desserts and to thicken gravy or soup. Form into cakes and fry in hot oil. Grate cooked manioc to make a base for fish cakes, cut into sections and fry in hot oil to make crisp chips. Put frozen manioc in boiling water or steam.

Food value manioc has more carbohydrate and less protein in it than other root vegetables. It is however quite a good source of vitamin C. Grated raw manioc makes a good porridge for infants and children when served with milk.

Okra

(Bhindi or Ladies' Fingers) The pods should be round, tender and of even color and about 3 inches (7 cm) long. Over-mature fruit are tough and stringy.

Store in plastic bags in a cool place. Lasts several days. Okra freezes well. Blanch in boiling water for 3 minutes, cool, dry and freeze. Alternatively, stir-fry 5 minutes in a little hot oil and cool, put prepared okra into plastic bags and freeze.

To use trim off short stems without cutting pod. If skin is very 'fuzzy' rib with nylon scraper under cold running water. To avoid sticky texture, sprinkle with vinegar and gently toss to ensure pods are well covered. Leave 30 minutes, wash well and dry. Boil whole in salted water and serve with butter or cold in salads. Cut into 1-inch (2-cm) lengths, mix with tomatoes and fry until tender. One of the main vegetables of curries and widely used in Middle Eastern cooking.

Food value a fair source of vitamins and minerals.

Papaya (Pawpaw)

Fruits should be firm and yellow in color. Select yellow or half-yellow fruits for ripening at home. Green fruit has a poor flavor. When ripened, flesh color and flavor differ according to variety. Size may vary from that of a grapefruit to a small watermelon. Flesh may be pink or orange in color and should be sweet.

Store ripe fruit in a cool place or refrigerator. Half-ripe fruit ripens in a dark cupboard. Freeze fruit purée.

To use cut into sections and scoop out seeds. Score flesh with a knife, sprinkle with lemon or lime juice. Peel ripe fruits, cut into cubes and use in fruit or vegetable salads. Do not add raw fruit to jellies as it contains a substance which breaks down gelatin. Use cooked papaya in pie, soufflé and mousse recipes. Blend ripe flesh to make papaya juice. Papaya is a good tenderizer for tough meat. Use green papaya as a vegetable.

Food value a rich source of vitamins C and A. A good first food for infants.

Passionfruit

Tropical passionfruit has a yellow shiny skin which becomes wrinkled on ripening.

Store in a cool place on wire racks. Fruits will keep a week in cool weather.

To use cut fruits in half and spoon out the pulp. Use the pulp with the seeds or strain. The pulp and seeds are used in fruit salads and cream-type desserts. The strained juice makes a very good fruit drink or addition to other fruit drinks and punches.

Food value a fair source of vitamins C and A.

Pineapple

Some varieties are yellow-orange when ripe while others are brownish green. Fruit must be firm all over with no sign of any damage or bruising as this will affect the texture and flavor.
Store ripe fruit in a cool place. It will last for 2-3 days. In hot weather put fruit into a plastic bag and refrigerate. Always cover cut fruit as it flavors other foods. Freezes well.
To use peel off outer skin. Remove eyes by cutting quarter-inch wedges diagonally along the lines of the eyes. Serve raw as a breakfast fruit or in fruit salads. Countless desserts and ice creams use pineapple as their principal fruit. Do not use raw fruit in gelatin dishes as it contains a substance which destroys gelatin. Pineapple slices or cubes are included in beef, pork or chicken recipes. Raw fruit will help tenderize meat and thus can be used in a marinade or as part of the recipe.
Food value a fair source of vitamin C.

Plantains

(Cooking bananas) The many varieties may be used green, half-ripe or ripe. Color of the flesh varies from cream to dark orange.
Store by hanging a bunch in a cool place or put 'hands' or loose fruit on a wire rack. Undamaged fruit will keep for several days. Ripening takes place during storage.
To use steam, boil or bake green fruits in the skin and peel before serving. Peel green fruit, slice thinly and fry in hot oil to make chips, or roast whole in hot fat around meat. To cook ripe fruits, bake, boil or steam in skin until soft. Remove skin, add coconut cream or grated coconut, simmer for a minute, then serve cold.
Food value similar to bananas. The orange-fleshed fruits are a good source of vitamin A.

Pomelo

This fruit is also known as Pummelo and Pamplemouse. It is a cross between a grapefruit and the tropical Shadock. Fruits can weigh up to a kilogram (2.2lbs) and more. When ripe, color varies between yellow and yellowish-green. The flesh is segmented, a little coarser than that of grapefruit, and varies in color from pale green to yellow or pale pink. Pomelos have a unique refreshing flavor.
Store on racks in a cool place. Fruits will last for two weeks in cool weather. Flavour and juiciness improve with storage. Freeze juice and make whole fruits into jams and marmalades.
To use peel off the skin and pith and eat segments raw. Cut in half and prepare as for grapefruit. Pomelo makes an excellent breakfast fruit. Remove segments and add to fruit salads or to shredded Chinese cabbage to make a salad. Squeeze out juice and make into drinks. Cut up half-ripe fruits and make into marmalade.
Food value a good source of vitamin C.

Rambutan

Has bunches of red or orange fruits, each looking like a large gooseberry covered in fleshy spines. The rind surrounds a melting white pulp and a seed. The fruit has an unusual sweet acid flavour.

Store on wire trays in a cool place or in perforated plastic bags in the refrigerator. Fruit has a short storage life at day temperatures.

To use cut the leathery rind with a sharp knife and pull back from the pulp. This fruit is best eaten fresh. The pulp can be included in fruit salads and ice creams.

Food value a good source of vitamin C.

Sapodilla

This fruit is also known as Sapodilla-plum, Zapote, Bully Tree and Naseberry. The medium-sized tree comes from South America and is now widely grown in tropical countries. It has round or oval, red-brown, thin-skinned fruits. When ripe, the fruit has a mass of luscious brown pulp which surrounds a large black seed.

Store mature fruits till soft and ripe on racks. Ripe fruits are best refrigerated.

To use Fruits should be soft. Peel the skin off ripe fruits and eat fresh. Remove the pulp and use to make ice creams and sorbets. It is important to ensure that the fruit is really ripe. Half-ripe fruits have a sticky consistency.

Food value a fair source of vitamins and minerals.

Soursop

Becomes very soft and the skin turns yellow during ripening. It is best to buy firm fruits and ripen at home. Soursop has a unique flavour which provides desserts and drinks with a distinctive taste.

Store in a cool place till soft. Soursop flesh and purée freezes well. Make into ice cubes.

To use cut in half and peel off soft skin. Rub through a wire strainer to make a thick purée or eat segments fresh. Do not break or eat the large black pips as these contain a toxic substance. Pour the purée over fruit salads. Use in fruit drinks, ice cream, sorbet and gelatin recipes. Combine with egg yolk to make custard. Thicken with a little cornflour, add lime juice and serve as a sauce for ice cream, fruit or cake desserts. Use to flavor whipped cream toppings or fillings. Serve as ice blocks in drinks.

Food value a good source of the vitamins riboflavin and niacin. Makes a good drink for children.

Sweet potato

(Kumara, kumala) Color varies from white to orange or purple. Always choose roots free from holes or rot. White varieties are less sweet than yellow. Purple roots have a very good flavor and texture.

Store in a dry airy place. Keeps for 2-3 weeks.

To use scrub well and steam, bake, or boil in skin. To avoid discoloration after peeling, put into cold water or cook in the skin and then peel. Serve with butter, sour cream and chives. To roast, parboil then peel and cook around meat or in hot fat. Very good with pork. Bake whole, scoop out flesh, season well with lemon juice or port wine, butter, salt and pepper. Refill shells and brown in hot oven. Cooked cubed sweet potato may be used to make salads. Include cooked purée in scones or soufflés. Make sweet potato pie from purée and rich egg custard baked in a pastry shell.

Food value a nutritious carbohydrate food. Good for infants. Yellow varieties provide vitamin A.

Tahitian Apple

This fruit is also known as Ambarella, Otaheite-apple, Wi or Vi apple, Great Hog Plum and Kedondong. It is an oval-shaped fruit and is picked when fully mature and green in color. On ripening the color changes to yellow. Crisp white flesh surrounds a spiny seed. The fruit has a refreshing sweet acid flavor.

Store on racks in a cool place or refrigerate. Fruits can ripen fast at day temperatures. For long storage, freeze cooked fruit or make juice into jelly or jam.

To use peel and cut up fruit to make into raw spicy chutneys or add to fruit salads. Cut up whole green fruits and boil with water till soft, strain off juice and make into jelly or jam. Rub cooked fruit through a sieve to make purée. This may be used in desserts or in a sauce to go with pork.

Food value a good source of vitamin C. The juice and puréed cooked fruit make good foods for small children.

Tangerine

Tangerines belong to the mandarin and orange family. The small round fruits are greenish yellow to bright orange in color and are widely grown in tropical areas of Southeast Asia. Fruits have a loose skin which is easily peeled off. They are very juicy and have a distinct aromatic flavor.

Store on racks in a cool place for a few days. Fruits soften quickly and for longer storage should be refrigerated. Juice and pulp freeze well. Half-ripe tangerines can be made into jam.

To use peel off the skin and separate segments. These are best eaten fresh. Squeeze out the juice to make drinks. Remove pith and seeds from segments and blend to make a purée. Use this in cold gelatin desserts, ice creams and sorbets.

Food value a good source of vitamin C.

Taro

(Dalo) The flesh of the many varieties ranges in color
from white to blue-grey. Texture may be fairly dry or
moist. Roots should be fresh and firm at the root end.
Store in a cool dry place. Keeps well for several days.
Alternatively, place unpeeled whole roots in a plastic bag
and seal. Roots will remain fresh for several months. Raw
peeled taro may be frozen.
To use bake in the skin or peel and bake whole or in
halves, slice and steam or boil. Put frozen pieces directly
in boiling water. Cooked taro makes excellent thick or
thin chips which remain crisp when cold. Add cubes of
prepared taro to fish dishes cooked in coconut cream.
Pound cooked taro to make a smooth dough, form into
1-inch (4-cm) balls or cubes. Serve with coconut cream or
caramel sauce as a dessert.
Food value a good carbohydrate food providing some
minerals, vitamins and protein.

Taro leaves

(Rouru) Pick only young leaves with green stems. Old
leaves and those from purple-stemmed varieties contain a
substance which irritates the mouth and throat. Some
leaves are free from this; in others it can be broken down
by rapid boiling in a closed pot.
To store wash and remove stems, put leaves together and
roll up. Put in a plastic bag in the refrigerator, or wrapped
in a banana leaf in a cool place. Keeps for several days.
To use cook leaves in boiling salted water for 5 minutes,
turn over and cook for another 5 minutes. Drain and add
butter or coconut cream. Put corned beef and chopped
onions on leaves, add coconut cream, wrap up and steam
or bake to make palusami. Use puréed leaves in cream
soups.
Food value a good source of vitamins C and A and
minerals. Provides some protein.

Tropical Squash

Varieties include Chinese marrow, long round, bottle,
lauki, luffa, taroi and others. One of the most interesting
and varied of vegetables.
Store on racks. Will keep for several days.
To use peel carefully, slice or dice and steam. Serve with
white or cheese sauce, or in curries. Round and long
squash can be stuffed by carefully cutting off the top,
removing seeds and stringy pith and filling with a
favourite meat or vegetable stuffing. Oven-bake till tender.
Grate or thinly dice crisp varieties and include in salads.
Dice and poach in a light syrup flavoured with lemon,
cloves, nutmeg or cinnamon and add to fruit salads, or use
as a stewed fruit. Sauté in hot butter with cubed pineapple
or apple, sweeten with brown sugar, add nutmeg or
cinnamon and serve hot or cold as a dessert.
Food value low nutritional value. Should be eaten with
legumes, milk, meat or fish.

Watermelon

Fruits are oval or round, and light green or darker variegated green. The flavor and color of the flesh depend on the fruit being mature. A mature fruit should sound hollow when lightly knocked. The inside flesh should be a bright pink color.

Store fruits in any airy cool place. Melons will keep for 4-5 days. Cut fruit should be put in a plastic bag in the refrigerator.

To use cut into slices and eat as fresh fruit. Cut into cubes or make into balls, flavor with lemon juice and mint and serve as a dessert, add to fruit salads, make into sorbet, use in gelatin desserts, cold fish dishes and vegetable salads. Blend to make a refreshing drink. Cut fruit in half, remove the flesh and use the shells as containers for fruit or vegetable salads. Use watermelon balls and cubes as a garnish for drinks, salads and desserts.

Food value watermelon has a low energy value and is a useful fruit for weight watchers.

Winged Beans

Beans should be soft; hard firm ones are not suitable for cutting and slicing. Beans vary from 4-6 inches (10-15 cm) in length.

Store in plastic bags in the refrigerator and use as soon as possible.

To use cut diagonally into slices and cook for 4-5 minutes in boiling salted water or stir-fry. Serve as for long beans. Cold winged beans make an excellent salad. Toss in a coconut cream dressing and flavor with chopped onion and tomato. Use the edible blue flowers as a garnish.

Food value a very good source of vitamins, minerals and protein. Because of their high food value, winged beans are known as a 'wonder food' of the tropics.

Yams

There are many varieties of yams ranging in size from 2-4 pounds (1-2 kg) to 50 pounds (25 kg) or more, and they may be white or purple in color. White yam is fairly similar to the potato in color and texture. Small sweet yams are 6-8 inches (15-20 cm) long. Most yams have a fine texture and flavor.

Store in a cool airy place. Roots will keep for many months under good conditions.

To use peel and slice and then steam or boil. To prevent browning, store peeled yams in water before cooking. Scrub whole yams and puncture before baking in the oven. Serve peeled and slice or scoop out flesh, grate or mash and season with butter, salt and pepper, return to shell and brown in oven. Add minced cooked meat and chopped parsley, cheese or flaked fish and coconut cream to mashed yam. Return to shell and bake. Roast pieces of peeled yam with meat.

Food value similar to taro. Mashed yam is a good infant food.